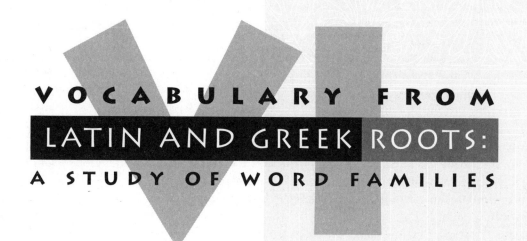

VOCABULARY FROM LATIN AND GREEK ROOTS:
A STUDY OF WORD FAMILIES

By: Elizabeth Osborne

Edited by Paul Moliken
Illustrated by Larry Knox

Prestwick House wishes to extend its gratitude to the many contributors whose assistance, comments, and expertise were essential in completing this book.

PRESTWICK HOUSE, INC.

"Everything for the English Classroom!"

P.O. Box 658 • Clayton, DE 19938
Tel: 1.800.932.4593 • Web site: www.prestwickhouse.com

ISBN-10: 1-58049-205-3
ISBN-13: 978-1-58049-205-8

INTRODUCTION

Prestwick House developed *Vocabulary from Latin and Greek Roots* in response to numerous requests for a solid etymology-based vocabulary program. Because the aim of the program is to increase retention of new words as well as to expand students' vocabulary, we chose to organize the units by meaning rather than alphabetically. A student who associates a root with an idea will be more likely to correctly assess the definition of that root's English derivative.

Each unit contains four Latin and/ or Greek roots; two to four English vocabulary words are provided for each root. Unit 14 of this book (p. 84), for example, includes four roots having to do with place, placing, or putting. When a student reaches the second root in this Unit, he or she will see the key letters that signal the presence of the root in an English word: POS. Beneath the key letters is the root from which the English is derived. Students will notice that there are sometimes two forms of the root, and sometimes one. The inclusion of two forms indicates a Latin verb from which English has taken two different forms. PONERE, for instance, gives us *component*, meaning "something put together with another thing to make a whole," while POSITUM gives us *deposit*, meaning "to put down."

When a root comes from a Latin adjective or noun, only one form will generally be included. Greek roots also appear in only one form.

Beneath the definition of the root, the student will find the word, its pronunciation, part of speech, and English definition. In cases in which an English word has multiple meanings, we have chosen to include only the meaning appropriate to the grade level for which the book is intended. The word *resignation* in this book, then, is a noun meaning "submission, surrender" rather than a formal withdrawal from a job or position; in Book III, *pedestrian* means "ordinary" rather than "a traveler on foot." In some instances, students may find it useful to review meanings that do not appear and discuss how they are related to the meaning presented.

If the word has a prefix, or if it is especially difficult to reconcile with its root, the entry will contain an analysis of the parts of the word, followed by a literal definition. *Repulsion* in Book III, Unit Five, is explained as *re*, meaning "back," + *pulsum*; the literal meaning is "a pushing back."

Finally, each entry provides a sentence using the word and introduces pertinent synonyms and/or antonyms. For added visual reinforcement of this understanding, mnemonic cartoons appear in each Unit.

Six different kinds of exercise follow the Unit entries. They include three kinds of practice using words in context, one test of a student's ability to infer information based on a word's meaning, one reading comprehension exercise, and one activity in which a student must deduce the meaning of an unfamiliar word based on knowledge of the word's root. By the end of the exercises in each Unit, students will have had thorough practice using the word in context and will be prepared to make the word part of their working vocabulary.

We hope that you find the *Vocabulary from Latin and Greek Roots* series effective in teaching new words and in fostering student interest in the history of our fascinating language.

Note: A guide to the pronunciation symbols and a list of Latin and Greek prefixes can be found at the beginning of this book.

PREFIXES

A (L.) away from

A(G.) not, no

AB (L.) away from

AD (L.)toward

ALTER (L.) another

AMPHI (G.) around, both

ANA (G.) up

ANTE (L.) before

ANTI (G.) against

CIRCUM (L.) around

CO (L.) with, together

CON (L.) with, together

CONTRA (L.) against

DE (L.) down, down from

DIA (G.) through

DIS (L.) apart, away from

DYS (G.) bad

E (L.) out of

EC (G.) outside

EM (G.) in, within

EN (G.) in, within

EPI (G.) upon

EX (L.) out of, away from *

HYPER (G.) over

IN (L.) in, into, on, against, not

INTRO (L.) inside

OB (L.) against

OMNI (L.) every, all

PER (L.) through

PERI (G.) around

POST (L.) after

PRE(L.) before

RE (L.) back, again *

RETRO (L.) backwards

SUB (L.) beneath

SUPER, SUR (L.) above

SYM (G.) with, together

SYN (G.) with, together

TRANS (L.) across

TELE (G.) distant

* Note: *Re, con, in,* and *ex* sometimes serve as *intensifiers*. In such cases, these prefixes simply mean *very*.

PRONUNCIATION GUIDE

a = tr<u>a</u>ck	o = j<u>o</u>b
ā = m<u>a</u>te	ō = wr<u>o</u>te
ä = f<u>a</u>ther	ô = p<u>o</u>rt
â = c<u>a</u>re	ōō = pr<u>oo</u>f
e = p<u>e</u>t	u = p<u>u</u>n
ē = b<u>e</u>	ū = <u>you</u>
	û = p<u>u</u>rr
i = b<u>i</u>t	
ī = b<u>i</u>te	ə = <u>a</u>bout, syst<u>e</u>m, s<u>u</u>pper, circ<u>u</u>s

WORD LIST FOR BOOK VI

UNIT 1
alacrity
assay
celerity
cogent
exigent
incite
intransigent
perturb
resuscitate
solicitous
turbid
turbulent

UNIT 2
cognate
degenerate
engender
feign
fictive
genre
innate
nascent
parturient
repertory
transfigure

UNIT 3
demise
diabolical
emblematic
episodic
hyperbole
inveigh
methodical
remit
surmise
synod
vehement

UNIT 4
aggregate
agrarian
bucolic,
egregious
fruition
fruitless
gregarious
idyllic
pastoral
peregrination
repast
rustic

UNIT 5
abscond
aperture
apocryphal
context
covert
cryptic
overt
pretext
recondite
subtext

UNIT 6
adjourn
anachronism
chronicle
demur
demure
diurnal
extemporaneous
moratorium
sojourn
synchronous
temporal
temporize

UNIT 7
animadversion
aspire
concordance
conspire
discordant
esprit
inanimate
psychotic
pusillanimous
pysche
pyschosomatic
transpire

UNIT 8
concede
concur
discursive
ensue
incessant
intercede
obsequious
perpetuate
perpetuity
segue
succor

UNIT 9
adjudicate
amoral
consecrate
execrable
expiate
impious
judicious
mores
morose
sacrosanct

UNIT 10
artifice
artless
emulate
icon
iconoclast
iconography
inert
inimitable
proviso
purveyor
purview

UNIT 11
inconsolable
incurious
innocuous
internecine
procure
salubrious
salutary
salutation
sinecure
solace

UNIT 12
conjugal
contiguous
contingent
defray
infrangible
refract
sectarian
subjugate
suffrage
transect

UNIT 13
adduce
capitulate
caprice
insuperable
precipitate
recapitulate
reserved
servile
sovereign
subdue
subservient
surfeit
traduce

UNIT 14
allocate
anathema
apposite
composite
dystopian
epithet
in lieu of
interpose
locus
topical
utopian

UNIT 15
ascribe
circumlocution
circumscribe
colloquy
consign
loquacious
magniloquent
obloquy
proscribe
resignation
signatory

UNIT 16
avocation
reticent
tacit
taciturn
univocal
verbatim
verbiage
verbose
vocation
vociferous

UNIT 17
adumbrate
apprise
comprise
discern
discrete
discretion
myopic
reprehensible
synopsis
umbrage

UNIT 18
complicit
confluence
dour
duplicitous
duress
explicate
flux
implicate
inexplicable
influx
irrepressible
obdurate
reprimand
suppress

UNIT 19
allude
collusion
derisive
felicitous
felicity
infelicitous
interlude
ludicrous
risible

UNIT 20
abstruse
adroit
constrain
incorrigible
intrusive
obtrusive
prestige
rectify
rectitude
stricture
stringent

UNIT 21
asset
devoid
evanescent
insatiable
plenary
plenipotentiary
satiety
vacuity
vacuous
vaunted

UNIT 22
attenuate
contend
distend
extenuating
ostensible
pertinacious
portend
tenable
tendentious
tenet
tenuous

UNIT ONE

AG, ACT
Latin AGERE, ACTUM "to drive, do"

COGENT (kō ´ jənt) *adj.* Strong and to the point; convincing
L. co (from con), "together," + actum = *driving together*
The defense attorney's claim that Brown was out of town during the murder was the most *cogent* argument that she had presented to date.
syn: convincing   *ant:* incoherent

EXIGENT (ek´ si jənt) *adj.* Urgent; pressing
L. ex, "out of," + agere = *driving out of*
The Congress held an impromptu all-night session to discuss the *exigent* threat of war.
syn: critical   *ant:* trivial

ASSAY (a sā´) *v.* To test, analyze
L. ex, "out of," + agere = *to drive out*
The miner *assayed* the cave soil for diamonds and gold.

INTRANSIGENT (in tran´sə jənt) *adj.* Refusing to compromise
L. in, "not," + trans, "across," + agere = *not driving across*
The principal was unable to come to a satisfying judgment in the teachers' debate, as the feuding faculty members were *intransigent*.
syn: stubborn   *ant:* obedient

The INTRANSIGENT TRANSIT bosses refused to make a compromise offer to the strikers.

⚏ *The word* assay *can mean "test or examine" in a broad sense, as in "to assay your knowledge," but the word usually applies to the kind of testing that determines the makeup of an ore or chemical substance.*

CIT
Latin CIEO, CITUM "to stir up, rouse"

INCITE (in sīt´) *v.* To stir up; to provoke
L. in, "strongly," + citum = *to strongly stir up*
Police were worried that the powerful and angry words of the speaker would *incite* the crowd to riot.
syn: urge   *ant:* soothe

RESUSCITATE (rē sus´ ə tāt) *v.* To bring back to consciousness
L. re, "again," + sub, "from beneath," + citum = *to rouse again from beneath*
The firefighters *resuscitated* a baby who had been overcome by smoke.
syn: revive

SOLICITOUS (sə lis´ə təs) *adj.* Showing care or worry
L. sollus, "whole," + citum = *stirring up the whole*
Barry's parents are *solicitous* because they have an immense amount of love for him.
syn: eager; concerned   *ant:* unconcerned

TURB
L. TURBARE, TURBATUM "disturb"

PERTURB (pər tûrb´) *v.* To make worried or upset
L. per, "through and through," + turbare = *thoroughly disturb*
It *perturbed* Lou when his daughter did not arrive home after school.
syn: bother   *ant:* calm

TURBULENT (tûr´ byə lənt) *adj.* Very excited or upset
The decade of the 1960's is considered by many scholars to be among the most *turbulent* in all of American history.
syn: agitated   *ant:* peaceful

TURBID (tûr´ bid) *adj.* Cloudy; confused
Gina's unclear ramblings are obviously the result of a *turbid* mind.
syn: muddled   *ant:* clear

ALACR
Latin ALACER "lively"

ALACRITY (ə lak´ ri tē) *n.* Enthusiastic quickness
When asked to evaluate a local store's ice cream, the boys responded with *alacrity* and happiness at the prospect.
syn: eagerness   *ant:* reluctance

CELER
Latin CELER "quick"

CELERITY (sə ler´ i tē) *n.* Speed or quickness
If the residential developments continue to grow with such *celerity*, local wetlands will be threatened.
syn: rapidity   *ant:* slowness

▥ *In Latin, French, and English, to "solicit" is to persistently approach someone with an offer, petition, or demand—to provoke (citum) him or her entirely (sollus). The English adjective solicitous, though, means something closer to "persistently seeking the care or well-being" of another person.*

▥ *The celer root also appears in the words accelerate (ad, "towards," + celer = towards speed), and decelerate (de, "down from," + celer = away from speed).*

EXERCISES - UNIT ONE

Exercise I. Complete the sentence in a way that shows you understand the meaning of the italicized vocabulary word.

1. The *turbid* waters of the river should have warned us that...

2. In response to the city's *exigent* financial situation, the Mayor...

3. The knights will *assay* the castle in order to...

4. Pictures of the flag being burned *incited* the crowd to...

5. The witness' *cogent* testimony prompted the jury to...

6. When asked to make a compromise, the most *intransigent* members of the political party...

7. Although paramedics tried for several minutes to *resuscitate* the woman, she...

8. Witnessing the car accident *perturbed* Dennis so much that...

9. The lawyer was *solicitous* towards the young family because...

10. The *celerity* with which the plant grew was amazing because...

11. Jana dealt with an especially *turbulent* period of her life by...

12. Rather than getting to her chores with *alacrity*, Helen...

Exercise II. Fill in the blank with the best word from the choices below. One word will not be used.

> solicitous   turbulent   celerity   perturb   cogent

1. Rather than allowing its characters to develop, the film moves with _____ to the gory shootout at the end.

2. If you act a bit more _____ towards your clients, they will understand that you really want to help them.

3. Marty's _____ account of his experiences during the war left the audience with a much clearer understanding of what had really happened.

4. Nothing will _____ Kathleen more than seeing someone be unkind to a child.

Fill in the blank with the best word from the choices below. One word will not be used.

> perturb   resuscitate   exigent   assay   turbulent

5. Because they were under extremely _____ circumstances, the committee took immediate action.

6. The troops defending the fort feared that a huge enemy force would _____ the defenses of the stronghold.

7. My Aunt Pearl fainted dead away, but we were soon able to _____ her.

8. The _____ emotions Jessie felt on a day-to-day basis sometimes left her exhausted.

Fill in the blank with the best word from the choices below. One word will not be used.

> turbid   exigent   alacrity   intransigent   incite

9. Even the most _____ sports-hater might be won over by the fast-paced excitement of extreme snowboarding.

10. Critics noted that the writer had once produced clear, delightful prose, but his poetry now was merely a(n) _____ and confusing stream.

11. On the day Ben had the good fortune to be assigned a report on his favorite musician, he set out for the library with _____.

12. Carefully chosen words in the pamphlets may _____ readers to stage a sit-in.

Exercise III. Choose the set of words that best completes the sentence.

1. During the _____ years following the war, angry leaders bent on further destruction would _____ their followers to demonstrate violently.
    A. intransigent; resuscitate
    B. solicitous; assay
    C. turbulent; incite
    D. turbid; perturb

2. After a few minutes of unconsciousness, Bernard opened his eyes to find a kindly and _____ nurse trying to _____ him with smelling salts.
    A. solicitous; resuscitate
    B. intransigent; assay
    C. turbulent; perturb
    D. exigent; incite

3.   Rather than offering a(n) _____ explanation of the basic principles of quantum physics, the author gives his readers only a few confusing, _____ paragraphs.
      A. turbid; solicitous
      B. solicitous; turbid
      C. exigent; cogent
      D. cogent; turbid

4.   Even when a crisis became so _____ that all the other firemen came close to collapsing under the stress, nothing seemed to _____ Chief Hornby.
      A. exigent; resuscitate
      B. cogent; assay
      C. intransigent; assay
      D. exigent; perturb

5.   The _____ jeweler absolutely refused to refund his customers' money, even after samples of his wares were _____ and found to contain only worthless fool's gold.
      A. perturbed; resuscitated
      B. turbulent; incited
      C. intransigent; assayed
      D. turbid; incited

Exercise IV. Complete the sentence by inferring information about the italicized word from its context.

1.   If Naomi deals with her clients in an *intransigent* manner, they will probably…

2.   When Professor Atwood gives her students a *cogent* explanation of a poem, the students will…

3.   If Eileen is *solicitous* towards the patrons who come into her library, she will probably get a reputation as…

Exercise V. Fill in the blank with the word from the Unit that best completes the sentence, using the root we supply as a clue. Then, answer the questions that follow the paragraphs.

When a new work of science fiction—be it movie, video game, novel, or television show—is released, there are always naysayers who disparage it. While they may find fault with the technical aspects of the work, the most _____ (TURB) aspect to them is the presence of extraterrestrial life. Many scientists argue that if something else were out there, we would have noticed it by now, and they criticize the application of human physical characteristics and emotions to aliens, citing the billion-to-one odds that life even occurred on Earth. Whether or not these arguments are true is up for debate; no one, after all, can expertly testify as to the appearance and behaviors of an alien race. What the critics fail to realize, though, is that the search for extraterrestrial life goes beyond technology and statistics; it speaks to humanity's innate need to seek out companionship.

Long before Galileo raised the first telescope to the night sky in 1609, humans asked themselves if they were alone in the universe. Early explorers setting out across deserts or oceans may have been looking for spices to trade and lands to conquer; inevitably, however, it was the new cultures they encountered that captured their spirits. Pioneers struggled to communicate and assimilate these "newly discovered" people into their own civilizations and to make their own communities larger and richer. Most important is that explorers never failed to bring back tales of their encounters with foreigners, to the amazement of audiences back home.

Now, without new earthbound territories to explore, the biggest mysteries lie in the stars. Only a select few are lucky enough to actually ascend into space, but that does not stop the rest of us from using our imaginations. And although we may have accepted that there is no man in the moon, why not contemplate the prospect of life on a planet hundreds, thousands, or millions of light-years distant?

In spite of the loud critics, not even science has given up on the potential for contact with other worlds. The existence of research projects devoted to searching for signs of extraterrestrial life (NASA's Origins Project and SETI, the Search for Extraterrestrial Intelligence, founded in 1984) is persuasive proof that the scientific community values the search. In fact, one of astronomy's most respected scientists, the late Carl Sagan, began the Planetary Society in part to _____(AG) theories about alien cultures.

Critics, therefore, should leave science fiction authors alone. Science fiction isn't necessarily about what's true and what we may know now. It's about the possibilities.

1. Which sentence best describes the view of the author?
    A. Alien life does exist.
    B. The early explorers mistakenly thought that the new people they encountered were aliens.
    C. Science fiction is not only about reporting the truth of alien life.
    D. Most scientists should believe that aliens have contacted us.

2. Why do many scientists object to the presence of alien life in science fiction?
    A. The physical characteristics are too disturbing to be real.
    B. The aliens often look and act too much like humans.
    C. Scientists don't believe aliens have technology more advanced than ours.
    D. The descriptions do not conform to what the experts know about alien life.

3. According to the essay, when did people start looking for alien life?
    A. in 1609, when Galileo invented the telescope
    B. in 1984, when SETI was started
    C. when there were no more new territories to explore on Earth
    D. People have always contemplated the possibility of aliens.

4. What is the purpose of mentioning Carl Sagan in the essay?
    A. The author wants readers to know that a respected scientist supported the search for extraterrestrial life.
    B. He is an expert on alien life who can attest to the characteristics of extraterrestrials.
    C. He is the most outspoken critic of science fiction novels.
    D. He is a pioneer in the study of cultural assimilation.

Exercise VI. Drawing on your knowledge of roots and words in context, read the following selection and define the *italicized* words. If you cannot figure out the meaning of the words on your own, look them up in a dictionary. Note that *os* means "mouth" and *re* means "back, again."

The first-year teacher began to question her skills when her normally energetic students began making *oscitant* gestures. "This," she said sternly, "may necessitate a *redaction* of the rules we drew up together at the beginning of the year." The revised rules did the trick, and her students stayed alert through the end of the semester.

UNIT TWO

GEN
Latin GENUS "race, type, kind"

DEGENERATE (dē jen´ ər et) *n.* A corrupt wrongdoer
L. de, "down from," + genus = *to fall from one's true nature or kind*
Most of the teachers at the school felt that Phil was a *degenerate* who could not
be trusted.
syn: ruffian

ENGENDER (en jen´ dər) *v.* To bring about; to produce
L. in, "in," + genus = *to bring into being*
The sudden rise in the cost of fuel *engendered* a high number of firings at the airline companies.
syn: beget   *ant:* prevent

GENRE (zhän´ rə) *n.* A kind or type of art
Frankenstein is a good example of a novel of the gothic *genre*.
syn: style

NASC, NAT
Latin NASCI, NATUS "to be born"

COGNATE (käg´ nāt) *adj.* Related to or coming from the same source
L. co, "together," + natus = *born together*
Linguists were baffled by the newly discovered language, which did not seem to
be *cognate* with any other they knew.
syn: related   *ant:* dissimilar

INNATE (i nāt´) *adj.* Natural; present from birth
L. in, "in," + natus = *inborn*
While other children needed lessons, Shirley Temple had an *innate* talent for
song and dance.
syn: intrinsic   *ant:* acquired

NASCENT (na´ sənt) *adj.* In the act of being born; growing
The President triumphantly announced that he had crushed a *nascent* rebellion in
his own political party before it could get out of control.
syn: developing   *ant:* mature

III *The living world is divided into seven scientific groups: kingdom, phylum, class, order, family, genus, and species. A genus of organisms contains all species of a particular type. For example, humans are of the genus "homo."*

FIG, FICT

Latin FINGERE, FICTUM "to shape"

TRANSFIGURE (trans fig´ yər) *v.* To change the form or appearance of
L. trans, "change," + fictum = *to change the shape of*
Building the Golden Gate Bridge *transfigured* the landscape of San Francisco.
syn: transform   *ant:* preserve

FICTIVE (fik´ tiv) *adj.* Not real
"Snow White and the Seven Dwarves" takes place in a *fictive* kingdom that captures children's imaginations.
syn: imaginary   *ant:* factual

FEIGN (fān) *v.* To make up or invent; pretend
Monica was easily able to *feign* shock, even though she knew about the surprise party in advance.
syn: fake

Although LANE FEIGNED a PAIN, his mother still sent him to school.

PAR, PER

Latin PERIRE "to give birth, produce"

PARTURIENT (pär tûr´ ē ent) *adj.* About to bring forth or give birth; pregnant
The naturalist wrote that the volcano before him seemed *parturient* with all the fires of Earth.

REPERTORY (rep´ ûr tôr ē) *n.* The range of works an artist can produce or perform
L. re, "back," + parere, "produce" = *produce back*
For such a young clarinetist, Rob has a surprisingly large *repertory*.

▥ *The English word repertory has a French counterpart, repertoire. Both come from the Latin reperire (re, "back," + perire = to produce back) meaning "to get back, to find out." A repertory (or a repertoire) is the body of works a person has mastered. Repertory can also refer to a standard set of plays a group of actors regularly performs in a theater, or the theater itself.*

EXERCISES - UNIT TWO

Exercise I. Complete the sentence in a way that shows you understand the meaning of the italicized vocabulary word.

1.   Fans wondered whether the runner's talent was *innate* or…

2.   Denise argued that most religions were not based on *fictive* notions, but rather…

3.   Because Fred was familiar with the *genre* of music, he…

4.   The jazz singer's full *repertory* included…

5.   Through his own efforts, Tom transformed himself from a *degenerate* into…

6.   When a democracy is *nascent*, it often…

7.   The holy man seemed to be *transfigured* by…

8.   Many weeks of talks between the two nations finally *engendered*…

9.   The children *feigned* interest in their father's story in order to…

10.   Researchers could tell that the words in one language were *cognate* with…

11.   Neil's *parturient* periods of withdrawal often ended in...

Exercise II. Fill in the blank with the best word from the choices below. One word will not be used.

degenerate   innate   genre   nascent   feign

1.   Mark, who had never enjoyed sports, was not able to _____ enthusiasm about the basketball game.

2.   Even though she had an unhappy childhood, Tamara never lost her _____ ability to find good in everything.

3.   No one _____ can contain the work of this multi-talented poet, musician, and painter.

4.   My _____ feeling of admiration for the artist soon grew into a strong emotional attachment.

Fill in the blank with the best word from the choices below. One word will not be used.

cognate   parturient   repertory   engender   innate

5.   Because the art forms are _____ with one another, we can assume they were originally one form.

6.   When roommates share a small apartment, extra courtesy can _____ harmonious relation-ships.

7.   Actors auditioning for the part are expected to have a full _____ of roles spanning modern American theater.

8.   The _____ pause gave way to a rush of shouted ideas and suggestions.

Fill in the blank with the best word from the choices below. One word will not be used.

transfigured   fictive   feigned   degenerate

9.   The otherwise ordinary painting was _____ into a stunning portrait by the afternoon light glowing around it.

10.   When some of the information submitted in court was found to be _____, a new trial had to be ordered.

11.   A longtime local _____ was picked up by police for cruelty to animals.

Exercise III. Choose the set of words that best completes the sentence.

1.   Oscar became a(n) _____ purely as a result of his hard life in the orphanage; violence and cru-elty are not _____ qualities in him.
   A.   genre; fictive
   B.   degenerate; nascent
   C.   degenerate; innate
   D.   cognate; innate

2.   The splitting of the original, ancient language into several dialects _____ several words that were _____ with one another.
   A.   engendered; nascent
   B.   transfigured; innate
   C.   engendered; cognate
   D.   feigned; fictive

3.   No matter how Diane tried to _____ love for Greg, she could not deny the _____ feel-ings of discontent and unhappiness that were growing within her heart.
   A.   engender; cognate
   B.   feign; cognate
   C.   feign; nascent
   D.   transfigure; innate

4. The religious ecstasy the poet felt seems to _____ the whole work; nothing else in this _____ of literature can come close to it.
    A. transfigure; genre
    B. feign; degenerate
    C. engender; degenerate
    D. feign; genre

5. The dancer's full _____ includes a complicated piece in which _____ stillness gives birth to frenzied movement.
    A. genre; nascent
    B. degenerate; parturient
    C. repertory; cognate
    D. repertory; parturient

Exercise IV. Complete the sentence by inferring information about the italicized word from its context.

1. If Ashley *feigns* boredom when her friend Jake talks about his upcoming fabulous vacation, we can infer that she…

2. When Frank, a well-known *degenerate*, sees a fight about to take place, we can expect him to…

3. When one word is *cognate* with another, both words probably…

Exercise V. Fill in the blank with the word from the Unit that best completes the sentence, using the root we supply as a clue. Then, answer the questions that follow the paragraphs.

It is an undeniable fact that Americans live in a consumer-driven society with a consumer-based economy. What many people do not realize, however, is how very destructive consumerism can be. Reckless spending on non-durable goods and services creates a direct and devastating effect on our health, our environment, and our financial well-being. Consumerism contributes to the decline of American culture by eating away at the very fabric of society.

The most obvious effect of rampant consumerism is its ruinous impact on our environment. Goods which are short-lived or even disposable are thrown into the trash bin without a second thought. Where does all this garbage go? Most of it sits decomposing in mammoth landfills in cities and towns across our country, polluting our air and taking up land which could be better used for constructive purposes. Because excessive consumerism _____ (GEN) the belief that everything is disposable, recycling efforts are, in effect, thwarted. Over 200 billion recyclable cans, bottles, plastic cartons, and paper cups are simply discarded each year, with no thought as to the consequences of their disposal.

Our environment faces an additional threat in the form of pollution from gas-guzzling vehicles like SUVs. The consumerist society, controlled in many ways by advertising, is driven to accept the notion that everything must be bigger, better, and faster, which is why Americans in particular manufacture and purchase the largest and least fuel-efficient vehicles in the world. Total dependence on the motor vehicle contributes extensively not only to air pollution, but also to the depletion of our natural resources.

Rampant consumerism also poses a considerable threat to our health and well-being. Advertising constantly hammers us with the fallacious idea that we must have instant gratification for all of our desires. When we are caught up in this _____ (FICT) notion of happiness without knowledge of or regard for the consequences, we continue to perpetuate a lifestyle of consumption and waste.

The future costs of these excesses, however, cannot be avoided. In addition to being detrimental to our health and our environment, consumerism is damaging to our financial well-being. Rampant spending on non-essential products causes severe financial distress. Whether due to credit card purchases, luxuries, or loans, many Americans live their lives constantly in debt.

Consumerism is a vicious cycle: we spend our

hard-earned money on the things that advertisers tell us we want or need, we work more in order to pay for these products, and all the while we are bombarded with more ads which increase our desire to acquire more things. In many ways, consumerism is the American dream distorted into the American nightmare.

1. Which of the following would be the most appropriate title for this passage?
   A. The Dangers of Capitalism
   B. The Destructive Power of Consumerism
   C. The Economic Impact of the Advertising Industry
   D. The Degeneration of American Society

2. Which of the following is the best definition of "consumerism," according to the passage?
   A. the act of buying expensive vehicles like SUVs
   B. rampant spending on unnecessary, non-durable goods
   C. the main tactic that advertisers use to get people to buy their products
   D. the inevitable outgrowth of a capitalist economy

3. Which of the following is *not* mentioned as an outgrowth of consumerism?
   A. pollution
   B. decline in societal well-being
   C. global warming
   D. credit card debt

4. According to the passage, recycling efforts are
   A. effective.
   B. thwarted.
   C. harmful.
   D. improving.

Exercise VI. Drawing on your knowledge of roots and words in context, read the following selection and define the *italicized* words. If you cannot figure out the meaning of the words on your own, look them up in a dictionary. Note that *carcino* means "cancer" and *pre* means "before."

Environmental law expert Erin Brockovich gained international recognition when she helped win a large lawsuit against chemical companies that placed harmful *carcinogens* in a town's drinking water. Brockovich was moved by the stories of the affected families, including many women whose children suffered from the after-effects of numerous *prenatal* diseases.

UNIT THREE

VEH
Latin VEHERE, VECTUM "to drag, to carry"

VEHEMENT (vē´ hə mənt) *adj.* Strongly emotional; fierce and passionate
Bob was *vehement* in his opposition to changing the company's marketing policy.
syn: intense   *ant:* indifferent

INVEIGH (in vā´) *v.* To attack strongly in words; to talk or write bitterly
against
L. in, "against," + vehere = *to drag against*
The preacher used his Sunday sermon to *inveigh* against the wretched morality of
his congregation.
syn: condemn   *ant:* praise

MIS
Latin MITTERE, MISUM "to send, to put"

Surmise comes to us from Latin via Old French. It was at one time a legal term meaning "to accuse" (literally to put [an accusation] on top of) and especially "to accuse without much cause." Out of the courts, it came to describe any conclusion not founded on reasonable cause.

SURMISE (sûr mīz) *v.* To draw a conclusion
based on little or no information; to   guess
L. super, "over, on top" + misum = *to put on top*
Although the prosecutor *surmised* that money
had motivated the killer, he had no evidence to
prove it.
syn: hypothesize   *ant:* prove

*The forecaster incorrectly SURMISED that today's
SUNRISE would happen at 6 AM.*

DEMISE (dē mīz´) *n.* The end of existence; death
L. de, "down," + misum, "sent" = *sent down*
Captain Redtooth spent his evenings plotting the *demise* of his hated nemesis.

REMIT (rē mit´) *v.* To make less or weaker; to forgive or pardon
L. re, "back," + mittere = *send back*
After a closer inspection of Hal's taxes, the IRS decided to *remit* the amount due.

BOL, BLEM
Greek BALLEIN "to throw, to cast"

EMBLEMATIC (em blə mat´ik) *adj.* Standing for another thing
G. em, "in," + ballein = *to throw in*
For immigrants to America, the Statue of Liberty was *emblematic* of the freedom and prosperity of the United States.
syn: symbolic   *ant:* unlike

DIABOLICAL (dī ə bäl´ ik əl) *adj.* Of or like a devil; very wicked or cruel
G. dia, "across," + ballein = *to throw across*
After splattering the class with red paint, little Rayna flashed a *diabolical* smile at her teacher.
syn: fiendish   *ant:* admirable

HYPERBOLE (hī pûr´ bəl lē) *n.* An exaggeration for effect
G. hyper, "above," + ballein, "throw" = *to throw above*
When Francine told us she would never speak to us as long as she lived, we assumed she was using *hyperbole*.

OD
Greek HODOS "road, way, coming"

EPISODIC (ep´ ə säd ik) *adj.* Happening in parts or segments
G. epi, "besides" + eis, "into," + hodos, "road" = *coming in besides*
Millions of viewers across the country tuned into the *episodic* reality TV hit series during its first season on the air.

METHODICAL (mə thäd´ i kəl) *adj.* Orderly and regular
G. meta, "beyond," + hodos = *way beyond*
To be an effective statistician, one must be a *methodical* worker who pays close attention to detail.

SYNOD (sin´ əd) *n.* A council, especially of churches or church officials
G. syn, "together," + hodos = *coming together*
Following the death of a Pope, the *synod* of bishops meets at St. Peter's Basilica to elect a new one.

III *A Greek* emblema *was a raised ornamental design which had been cast (ballein) in the surrounding material. In English, an* emblem *is that which stands apart, as the* emblema *stood out, and represents some other figure or quality. Something* emblematic, *then, is something representative or symbolic of something else.*

III *The Greek word* diabollein *originally meant "to hurl words across" or " to slander, accuse." When a Greek term was needed to translate the Hebrew* Satan *(literally, "accuser"),* diabollein *was the natural choice. As the Christian world added negative ideas to* Satan, diabolical *also came to be associated with terrible things. This, is also where we get the word* devil.

EXERCISES - UNIT THREE

Exercise I. Complete the sentence in a way that shows you understand the meaning of the italicized vocabulary word.

1.   I thought that Fred was employing *hyperbole* when he told me about the fish, but…

2.   A *synod* was called for the purpose of…

3.   John's *surmise* about who stole the car was based on…

4.   The marchers' protest of the brutal dictator was *emblematic* of…

5.   The dentist notified Greg that he would not *remit* changes for the root canal if…

6.   The *demise* of many local businesses was brought about by…

7.   The scheme thought up by the children was so *diabolical* that…

8.   Geraldine was so *vehement* in her defense of her friend that…

9.   Monica's bouts of coughing had once been *episodic*, but they now…

10.   When the police chief *inveighed* against the mayor, the mayor…

11.   Terence's *methodical* arrangement of his baseball cards showed that he…

Exercise II. Fill in the blank with the best word from the choices below. One word will not be used.

emblematic   diabolical   vehement   demise   hyperbole

1.   In a voice that grew more and more _____, Danny insisted that he had not been present on the night of the crime.

2.   Since callers to the emergency line often used _____ to describe their injuries, the medical staff tended not to take them seriously.

3.   Television may be bad for society, but has it really brought about the _____ of our culture?

4.   Nothing is more _____ of the success of international trade than the thriving marketplace in the center of the city.

Fill in the blank with the best word from the choices below. One word will not be used.

diabolical   episodic   remitted   surmised   inveigh

5.   The _____ nature of the author's poems makes it easy to spot recurring patterns and cycles.

6.   From the disorderly state of the room, Anita _____ that the children had been roughhousing again.

7.   When the investigative reporter looked more closely into the crime, she found a conspiracy so _____ that it made her hair stand on end.

8.   The orator knew that choosing to _____ against the Emperor would mean certain death.

Fill in the blank with the best word from the choices below. One word will not be used.

vehement   methodical   synod   remit

9.   If you _____ the lawyer's fee before the trial, you will receive reimbursement after the case is settled in your favor.

10.   George continued to work in his slow, _____ way, never deviating from the list in front of him.

11.   It fell to the _____ to issue rules governing the whole Church.

Exercise III. Choose the set of words that best completes the sentence.

1.   Tiffany hoped that her _____ protest of the new smoking ban would bring about the _____ of a government she considered corrupt and untrustworthy.
    A.   methodical; hyperbole
    B.   vehement; synod
    C.   vehement; demise
    D.   methodical; synod

2.   The Senator _____ against the Prime Minister for hours, calling him a(n) _____ tyrant and a cold-blooded murderer.
    A.   inveighed; diabolical
    B.   remitted; synod
    C.   surmised; methodical
    D.   remitted; diabolical

3.   Because Julia rarely used _____, when she told us about what she had found at the crime scene, we _____ that something truly terrible had happened.
    A.   surmise; remitted
    B.   hyperbole; surmised
    C.   synod; inveighed
    D.   surmise; inveighed

4.   Dave's boss criticized him for being too strict and _____, saying that such lack of creativity was
      _____ of the problems in the company as a whole.
      A.   episodic; emblematic
      B.   emblematic; methodical
      C.   diabolical; methodical
      D.   methodical; emblematic

5.   The _____ called by the Czar voted unanimously not to _____ church monies to France.
      A.   synod; surmise
      B.   hyperbole; inveigh
      C.   synod; remit
      D.   demise; remit

Exercise IV. Complete the sentence by inferring information about the italicized word from its context.

1.   If Bebe frequently uses *hyperbole*, her friend may begin to...

2.   Doug was *vehement* about stopping to help the stranded motorists; we suspected it was because...

3.   When the twins heard of the *demise* of their favorite band, they probably...

**Exercise V. Fill in the blank with the word from the Unit that best completes the sentence, using the root
      we supply as a clue. Then, answer the questions that follow the paragraphs.**

Fidel Castro, ruler of Cuba, began his bid for power with a simple and laudable goal: to utilize a mass movement for social change to better the people of Cuba.

The 1950's were a turbulent time for Cuba. As Castro readied himself to campaign for a seat in Cuba's parliament, he watched General Fulgencio Batista overthrow the elected government. Early in Batista's dictatorship, Castro was a vocal opponent of the General's policies. Using his legal training, Castro petitioned Cuba's Supreme Court, claiming Batista's government was in violation of the Cuban constitution.

After the petition was denied, Castro began a more confrontational approach, organizing attacks on Batista and his regime; this eventually got him arrested. After serving two years in prison for the attacks, he was released in a general amnesty. When peaceful methods of protest again failed, Castro retreated to Mexico in a self-imposed exile. A few years later, though, he returned to Cuba with limited troops and supplies; from then on he _____(OD) and continuously used guerrilla warfare to attack the Batista regime. Without foreign support, the regime soon fell, Batista fled the country, and Castro was recognized as a strong leader, but one with unknown political agendas.

The new government under the control of Fidel Castro began with moderate policies and governmental leaders. In fact, Castro's government was recognized and supported by the United States. However, the _____(MIS) of the new international relationship came quickly, as Castro began initiating more nationalistic, radical, and confrontational policies.

In 1960, Castro seized and nationalized all American-owned and other foreign-held property. He further infuriated his former Western international supporters when he signed oil deals with the Soviet Union. Even faced with _____(VEH) opposition, Castro insisted that Cuba would remain a communist country. With a breakdown in diplomatic relations and two crucial events, the Bay of Pigs invasion and the Cuban Missile Crisis, strained relations between the United States and Cuba escalated into hostility. Even as Cuba was being isolated from the United States, though, the people of Cuba, whose lives and living conditions had improved, rallied behind their leader and gave Castro their full support.

Cuba has continued to experience change in past years. Because it was so dependent on the Soviet Union, Cuba's economy was directly affected by the USSR's collapse in the 1990's. Cuban refugees have been a thorny issue, as each year many try to enter the United States illegally by fleeing the island. In the decades since Castro became the Cuban leader, he has been portrayed as both a(n) _____ (BOL) dictator and a charming communist.

1. Which sentence below best sums up the main idea of the passage?
    A. Fidel Castro opposed Fulgencio Batista's policies.
    B. Fidel Castro employed both peaceful and military strategies in gaining power and governing Cuba.
    C. The United States and Cuba are mutually hostile.
    D. Communism is a superior governmental philosophy found throughout the world.

2. Why did the Cuban economy begin to face economic hardship in the 1990's?
    A. The United States did not support the regime of Fidel Castro.
    B. Prestigious Cubans were fleeing Cuba to live in the United States.
    C. The world economy was facing increasingly troubled times.
    D. The collapse of the Soviet Union affected its communist associates.

3. According to the article, Castro entered the political arena because
    A. he opposed the United States.
    B. he wanted to win Cubans over to his cause.
    C. he was opposed to the manner in which Batista came into power.
    D. he disliked Cuba's relationship with the United States.

4. According to the author, the Cuban people supported Castro because
    A. he was willing to stand up to the superpowers.
    B. he became an even more powerful dictator than Batista.
    C. he was able to better the living conditions for the masses.
    D. he was responsible for ending the Batista regime.

Exercise VI. Drawing on your knowledge of roots and words in context, read the following selection and define the *italicized* words. If you cannot figure out the meaning of the words on your own, look them up in a dictionary. Note that *in* means "against" and *peri* means "around."

Ted went to a marriage counseling center and started to shout *invective*. His past experiences with women and relationships left him with a strong hatred of what he called "an institution of evil." *Periodically*, he jumped up and made punching motions at the wall, demonstrating his anger.

UNIT FOUR

⚏ *In ancient Greece and Rome, a long tradition of literature was founded on an idealized notion of country life. This genre is often broadly referred to as* pastoral, *and it covers several forms of prose and both short and long verse. An* idyll, *for instance, is a short work describing one incident or scene in a rural setting. The most famous* idylls *are by the Greek poet Theocritus. Other important ancient pastoral works include those by the Greek Longus and the Roman poet Virgil. English poets picked up the theme, especially in the sixteenth and seventeenth centuries. John Milton, Edmund Spenser, and even William Shakespeare drew on pastoral imagery and forms.*

PAST
Latin PASCERE, PASTUS "to feed (especially flocks or herds)"

PASTORAL (pâ´ tər əl) *adj.* Having to do with the country
Poet William Wordsworth's works often evoke images of the *pastoral* English countryside.

REPAST (rē past´) *n.* A meal; food and drink for a meal
L. re, "again," + pastus = *feed again*
Because he was on a diet, Josh could not enjoy the bounties of the great *repast* prepared for Christmas.
syn: feast

GREG
Latin GREX, GREGIS "herd, flock"

AGGREGATE (ag´ rə gət) *adj.* Gathered into a whole; total
L. ad, "towards," + gregis = *towards the herd*
The economist gave the board of directors an interesting presentation on *aggregate* demand for the company's goods.
syn: combined   *ant:* individual

EGREGIOUS (e grē´ jəs) *adj.* Standing out sharply as wrong or bad
L. ex, "out of," + gregis = *out of the herd*
The feud between the station and the show's producers was based on an *egregious* error in an important report.
syn: glaring   *ant:* minor

GREGARIOUS (grə ger´ ē əs) *adj.* Liking to be with other people
The most important thing to have for a customer service job was a *gregarious* personality.
syn: social   *ant:* unfriendly

AGRI
Latin AGER "field"

AGRARIAN (ə grer´ ē ən) *adj.* Having to do with farming
In the early stages of our nation's development, the economy was primarily *agrarian*.
syn: agricultural   *ant:* urban

The LIBRARIAN cares about farmers and other AGRARIAN affairs.

PEREGRINATION (per ə gri nā´ shən) *n.* The act of traveling about; a journey
L. per, "through," + ager = *through the fields*
Johnny Appleseed's *peregrination* through the early United States has been the subject of many legends.
syn: journey

FRUI
Latin FRUI, FRUITUS "to enjoy, to harvest"

FRUITION (frōō ish´ un) *n.* Fulfillment of an effort or desire
The dreams of many people came to *fruition* on the day the railroad was completed.
syn: realization   *ant:* frustration

FRUITLESS (frōōt´ lis) *adj.* Yielding no positive results
Ken's many hours filling out job applications were *fruitless*, landing him no lucrative employment offers.
syn: in vain   *ant:* successful

RUS
Latin RUS, RURIS "country"

RUSTIC (rus´ tik) *adj.* Having to do with the countryside; rural
L. rus, "countryside"
The *rustic* charm of the shepherd's little cottage made us want to stay in the country forever.

COL
Greek KOLOS "herdsman"

BUCOLIC (byōō käl´ ik) *adj.* Having to do with country life or farms
G. bous, "cow," + kolos, "herder" = *cow-herder*
The family was forced to make the switch from the *bucolic* tranquility of their farm to the hectic city life of New York.

ID
Greek EIDOS "form, shape, little work of verse"

IDYLLIC (ī dil´ ik) *adj.* Simple and pleasant
G. eidyllion, "little form"
Until the end of his life, Peter treasured the memory of his *idyllic* holiday in the mountains.

EXERCISES - UNIT FOUR

Exercise I. Complete the sentence in a way that shows you understand the meaning of the italicized vocabulary word.

1.   Rather than the *idyllic* village she had expected, Maureen found Brownsville to be...

2.   The volunteers at the animal shelter knew that their efforts had not been *fruitless* when...

3.   The *pastoral* themes of the poem included...

4.   The most *egregious* error made by the quiz-show contestant resulted in...

5.   Ben was the most *gregarious* employee of the library, and could often be seen...

6.   The author claims that his book took years to come to *fruition* because...

7.   The cabin's *rustic* appeal came through in details like...

8.   The *bucolic* setting of the little town inspired many poems about...

9.   The meeting focused on *agrarian* issues, such as...

10.   *Aggregate* sales for the year must be calculated differently than...

11.   The family's frequent *peregrinations* resulted in...

Exercise II. Fill in the blank with the best word from the choices below. One word will not be used.

egregious   rustic   agrarian   gregarious   fruitless

1.   A more _____ person would have been eager to meet everyone at the party, but Wendell, a shy child, hung back.

2.   Ray, who had spent his life in the big city, was now in search of a more _____ lifestyle.

3.   Abbie feared that her efforts to build a playground for the children might be _____, leaving them with the same trash-strewn vacant lot they had had for years.

4.   Because the population is largely _____, it has needs that are different from those of the city-dwellers an hour away.

Fill in the blank with the best word from the choices below. One word will not be used.

repast   peregrination   pastoral   aggregate   fruition

5.   The play opens in a(n) _____ setting, complete with sheep and hay bales.

6.   To celebrate the athlete's success, the town held a grand _____ and invited everyone to dine.

7.   Since talks between the divorcing couple were clearly not coming to _____, their lawyers decided to meet in court.

8.   The poet's _____ in the isolated northern desert led him to write a book of verses on travel.

Fill in the blank with the best word from the choices below. One word will not be used.

bucolic   gregarious   aggregate   idyllic

9.   We enjoyed a(n) _____ holiday in the countryside of Ireland.

10.   Hazel enjoyed the _____ loveliness of the fields of speckled cattle.

11.   The _____ results of the national census were roughly similar to the census results by state.

Exercise III. Choose the set of words that best completes the sentence.

1.   The _____ splendor of the farm that we visited convinced us to adopt a more _____ life-style.
    A.   agrarian; gregarious
    B.   egregious; agrarian
    C.   aggregate; gregarious
    D.   pastoral; agrarian

2.   A(n) _____ error was made at the royal _____; the king was allowed to dine on spoiled food.
    A.   egregious; repast
    B.   pastoral; agrarian
    C.   idyllic; repast
    D.   bucolic; peregrination

3.   Being a naturally _____ person, the mail carrier made many friends on his _____ through the country and town.
    A.   idyllic; peregrinations
    B.   aggregate; agrarians
    C.   gregarious; peregrination
    D.   bucolic; fruitions

4. The developer's attempts to build a new shopping center on the farmland were _____ because local residents wanted to preserve the area's _____ character.
    A. rustic; aggregate
    B. fruitless; idyllic
    C. idyllic; gregarious
    D. aggregate; idyllic

5. Even the _____ pressure of all the citizens combined could not make the public works project come to _____.
    A. aggregate; fruition
    B. idyllic; peregrination
    C. fruitless; repast
    D. egregious; repast

Exercise IV. Complete the sentence by inferring information about the italicized word from its context.

1. In response to the *egregious* mistake in Gwyn's essay, her teacher will probably…

2. When speaking of his birthplace, Anthony describes a *pastoral* setting, complete with…

3. When Polly, the *gregarious* valedictorian of this year's graduating class, is surrounded by cheering class-mates, she may do things like…

Exercise V. Fill in the blank with the word from the Unit that best completes the sentence, using the root we supply as a clue. Then, answer the questions that follow the paragraphs.

The next time you walk through the produce section of your local supermarket, think about the chemicals and pesticides lurking on those luscious-looking fruits and veg-etables. Each year, American farmers layer tons of pesticides and chemicals onto our agricultural farmland, and no one really knows the long-term health effects of ingesting that tainted produce.

The return to organic farming that we have seen in the last few years is a response to these concerns. In fact, organic farming is at the forefront of the new _____ (AGRI) revolution. California farmer David Masumoto is one of a growing number of organic farming revolutionar-ies. He says that he wants everyone to know what tasting a great peach is really like. A devotee of organic farming, he gives the consumer the opportunity to buy healthy, tasty, organic produce. Masumoto favors working in harmony with nature rather than overpowering the environment with chemicals and pesticides. He avoids the potential harm of pesticides to his land and his products through his organic farming methods.

Due to legislation and the dedication of farmers such as David Masumoto, consumers today can take advantage of a greater abundance of organic fruits and vegetables. There certainly are compelling reasons to try. The family that "goes organic" will be much healthier, since no one will need to worry about pesticide poisoning. An added benefit is that any _____(PAST) of organic fruits and vegetables will always be more satisfying. It will be a new adventure to discover how produce really was meant to taste.

The organic farming scene is much closer to the fam-ily farm of earlier times in which man and nature mutu-ally coexisted in a more peaceful setting than the general factory-type agribusiness farm of today. Organic farmers maintain that a natural approach to farming does not pol-lute the land; instead it leaves the air pure, without clouds of chemicals and pesticide sprays.

The benefits for the consumer are numerous. The California Department of Pesticide Regulation found in a ten-year study (1989-1998) that fifty-four percent of all conventional (non-organic) fruits and vegetables had pesti-cide residues. This telling statistic is diametrically opposed to the fact that in the same sample, only seven percent of the certified organic produce contained pesticides.

1.   According to this article, a person should choose organic produce in order to
      A. save the environment.
      B. keep farmers in business.
      C. reap the health benefits.
      D. keep the air pure.

2.   The main idea of this passage is that
      A. organic farming is safer for people and the environment.
      B. organic farming is more expensive and time-consuming.
      C. the government opposes organic farming through regulations.
      D. most farmers today are practicing organic farming.

3.   According to the passage, organic farming
      A. is a new invention.
      B. can be linked to earlier times.
      C. was invented by David Masumoto.
      D. is very unpopular today.

Exercise VI. Drawing on your knowledge of roots and words in context, read the following selection and define the *italicized* words. If you cannot figure out the meaning of the words on your own, look them up in a dictionary. Note that *nomy* means "study of a particular field" and that *se* means "apart."

Agronomy and plant genetics have come together in the new science of strategical bio-farming. Manipulation of a *segregant* gene has allowed for production of a hearty new strain of corn which can resist diseases and weather damage. The separation of the chromosomes in the original gene was accidentally achieved in a lab, but can now be brought about intentionally. Once the genetically different corn is available in seed form, the soil that supports it must be tested and monitored so that the highest yield is possible.

UNIT FIVE

COND
Latin CONDERE, CONDITUM "hide, put away"

ABSCOND (ab skänd´) *v.* To leave in a hurry, especially to escape the law
L. ab, "away," + conditum = *hide away*
Vincenzo *absconded* with the Mona Lisa under his coat.
syn: flee

RECONDITE (rek´ ən dīt) *adj.* Difficult to understand; hidden from
        understanding
L. re, "back," + conditum = *hidden back*
Paula, an art major, found political science a *recondite* subject.
syn: obscure   *ant:* accessible

CRYPT
Greek KRYPTEIN "to hide"

CRYPTIC (krip´ tik) *adj.* Hard to understand; having a secret meaning
The code expert spent hours attempting to decipher the letter's *cryptic* message.
syn: unclear   *ant:* obvious

APOCRYPHAL (ə päk´ rə fəl) *adj.* Coming from an unreliable source; untrue
G. apo, "away," + kryptein = *hidden away*
Though many people believe it as fact, the tale of George Washington and the
cherry tree is completely *apocryphal*.
syn: unauthenticated   *ant:* accurate

▥ *The* Apocrypha *is the
name given to certain
books of the Bible which
are accepted by some
churches, but rejected as
false by others.*

ERT
Latin APERIRE "uncover," OPERIRE "cover"

APERTURE (ap´ ər chər) *n.* An opening or a hole
L. aperire, "uncover"
An *aperture* in the wall let us peer through into the garden.

OVERT (ō vûrt´) *adj.* Public, unhidden; open
L. aperire, "uncover"
Presidents have become more *overt* in their decision-making since the Nixon era and the Watergate investigation.
syn: observable   *ant:* disguised

COVERT (kō vûrt´) *adj.* Done in a hidden or secret manner
L. co, "strongly," + operire = *strongly cover*
The CIA is known for its *covert* operations and missions.
syn: stealthy   *ant:* aboveboard

The spy was caught when his COVERT observation was UNCOVERED.

TEXT

Latin TEGERE, TEXTUM "weave, cover"

CONTEXT (kon´ tekst) *n.* The circumstances or setting surrounding an event
L. con, "together," + textum = *woven together*
In order for us to truly understand the novel, we need to know the *context* in which it was written.

SUBTEXT (sûb´ tekst) *n.* The hidden or underlying meaning of something
L. sub, "beneath," + textum = *woven beneath*
Readers searching for a political *subtext* in the novel will exhaust themselves listing the possible references to modern events.

PRETEXT (prē´ tekst) *n.* A stated reason for doing something; an excuse
L. pre, "before," + textum = *woven before*
Dictators often use national unity as a *pretext* for oppressing all opposition groups.
syn: ploy

Ⅲ Integument (*in, "on,"* + *tegere = cover on*) *is a word meaning "skin or outer covering."*

EXERCISES - UNIT FIVE

Exercise I. Complete the sentence in a way that shows you understand the meaning of the italicized vocabulary word.

1.   People examining the *subtext* of a debate will often find...

2   Callie showed *overt* hostility towards Michael when she...

3.   Even though Lucy's warning to Kyle was rather *cryptic*, Kyle...

4.   The religious figure spoke about matters so *recondite* that...

5.   An *aperture* in the telescope allowed observers to...

6.   Through *covert* activities, the small group of soldiers could...

7.   Many journalists believed the President's story about the secret meeting was *apocryphal* because...

8.   In order to provide a *context* for the story about her first dog, Leigh told her listeners...

9.   Merle and Kevin *absconded* with the mascot's costume in order to...

10.   Carl's *pretext* for asking Mario such nosy questions was...

Exercise II. Fill in the blank with the best word from the choices below. One word will not be used.

recondite   apocryphal   cryptic   overt

1.   Even though Willie did not show a(n) _____ dislike for his new coworker, I could tell he was displeased.

2.   There seems to be no area of knowledge so _____ that Professor Moyo does not know something about it.

3.   Because the words of the song were rather _____, Harold had a hard time figuring out what the song actually meant.

Fill in the blank with the best word from the choices below. One word will not be used.

pretext   apocryphal   covert   subtext

4.   Until there is physical proof of the existence of UFO's, the tales people relate of encounters with aliens should be considered _____.

5.   Close observers may discover a sinister _____ beneath much of the author's innocent-seeming narrative.

6.   Several top-level executives were discovered making _____ deals and releasing highly secret information.

Fill in the blank with the best word from the choices below. One word will not be used.

apertures   subtexts   pretext   context   absconded

7.   In order to avoid the angry crowd calling for his arrest, Patrick _____ in the dead of night.

8.   Cynthia did not even bother to provide a(n) _____ as to why she was leaving the house at midnight.

9.   Both _____ of the camera were blocked, so that the photographer could not look through the lens.

10.   Without some _____, the subject of the odd painting will make no sense to a modern-day viewer.

Exercise III. Choose the set of words that best completes the sentence.

1.   In order to _____ with top-secret military information, the scientist chose only the most _____ methods of travel.
      A.   abscond; covert
      B.   abscond; overt
      C.   recondite; apocryphal
      D.   cryptic; covert

2.   Although the principal showed _____ displeasure with the students who had started the fire, his speech to them was _____ and confusing.
      A.   recondite; apocryphal
      B.   cryptic; recondite
      C.   overt; cryptic
      D.   apocryphal; cryptic

3.   The information sought by the secret agents was so _____ that they had no way of knowing whether certain stories were _____ or true.
      A.   recondite; apocryphal
      B.   covert; cryptic
      C.   overt; recondite
      D.   apocryphal; overt

4.   Like a(n) _____ in a telescope, the critic's writings provide a new glimpse of the formerly hidden
      _____ of the play.
      A.   pretext; aperture
      B.   aperture; subtext
      C.   recondite; subtext
      D.   context; aperture

5.   Needing a _____ for attacking the neighboring country, the king said he had intercepted _____
      messages from enemy spies.
      A.   subtext; overt
      B.   pretext; apocryphal
      C.   pretext; covert
      D.   context; cryptic

Exercise IV. Complete the sentence by inferring information about the italicized word from its context.

1.   If an *apocryphal* story about killer bees begins to spread in Brownsville, Brownsville residents should
      probably…

2.   Paula is *covert* in her visits to the nightclub; it may be the case that…

3.   Whoever *absconded* with the heavy box of computer supplies probably…

**Exercise V. Fill in the blank with the word from the Unit that best completes the sentence, using the root
      we supply as a clue. Then, answer the questions that follow the paragraphs.**

In 1922, an archaeologist named Howard Carter led an expedition to the Valley of the Kings in Egypt. With the financial backing of Lord Carnarvon, a wealthy British nobleman, Carter searched for the long-hidden tomb of Pharaoh Tutankhamen. Little was known about the youthful king, but Carter had sought the location of the tomb for years, knowing that the Pharaoh and his treasure lay hidden somewhere within the valley, possibly undisturbed. Robbers had plundered many tombs, and _____ (COND) with both the mummies and their riches, despite ominous curses protecting the pharaohs' graves.

Many of Egypt's rulers had been entombed in the Valley of the Kings. They were mummified and buried along with necessities for the afterlife and caches of valuables, thus making their tombs known targets for thieves. In an effort to prevent robbery, ancient architects designed secret passageways in the tombs to deter and confuse any would-be thieves. The burial chambers were protected by curses in the form of inscriptions warning of the dangers befalling anyone who disturbed the kings. These threats ranged from disappearance to misery to death. Outsiders dismissed these curses, but many Egyptians accepted them as credible truths. As a result, archaeologists encountered great obstacles retaining workers who were undaunted by the curses and their alleged consequences.

King Tut's tomb was no exception to the ubiquity of the pharaohs' curses. By some accounts, a curse appeared over a door; others described an engraved slate (which later mysteriously disappeared) warning of death to those who entered the tomb. Furthering the notion of curses, a series of _____ (CRYPT) events surrounded the tomb's opening.

Howard Carter had used a pet canary to locate King Tut's tomb. On the very day that he revealed his discovery, though, a snake, thought by the ancient Egyptians to be a messenger from the afterlife, bit and killed the canary. Shortly thereafter, Lord Carnarvon, who had financed the mission, died of an infected insect bite. Two other mysterious incidents, which gave more credence to the theory of a curse, occurred at the same moment as Carnarvon's death: Carnarvon's beloved dog, at home in England, died, and the city of Cairo lost power. According to believers, each peculiar event was an _____ (ERT) example attributed to the mummy's curse, and, understandably, Tut's tomb became shrouded in fear. Still more stories surfaced describing mysterious deaths of workers at the site, and the curse became regarded as formidable and genuine.

Even years later, people continue to speculate about the

causes of the numerous inexplicable deaths attributed to Tut's curse and similar curses found at other burial sites. Scientists, however, have discovered a possible explanation for the deaths. Dangerous bacteria have been found inside ancient tombs; when stirred up by movement, the bacteria can be inhaled, resulting in illness and even death. Perhaps this might explain what earlier generations believed were messages from the long-dead pharaohs.

1. Which sentence best states the main idea of this passage?
    A. Howard Carter fulfilled a lifelong dream when he unearthed the tomb of King Tut.
    B. The mystery surrounding the pharaohs and their tombs led to fear and misunderstanding.
    C. When robbers plundered ancient tombs, they stole vital clues that would solve the mystery of the curses.
    D. The scientific community strongly disagrees regarding the credibility of the mummy's curse.

2. What was Lord Carnarvon's role in the discovery of King Tut's tomb?
    A. He led the expedition.
    B. He researched the location of the tomb.
    C. He provided the tools and the workforce.
    D. He provided the financial backing.

3. Why were curses placed upon the tombs?
    A. to forestall robbers who might disturb the bodies
    B. to maintain the secret locations of the tombs
    C. to hinder explorers
    D. to create an atmosphere of mystery

4. What, according to the passage, may explain the deaths surrounding the discovery of King Tut's tomb?
    A. Many of the workers were exhausted and weakened from dehydration.
    B. Workers inhaled toxic bacteria inside the tomb.
    C. Those people became victims of the curse's power.
    D. Those people were victims of an elaborate hoax designed to foster belief in the mummy's curse.

Exercise VI. Drawing on your knowledge of roots and words in context, read the following selection and define the *italicized* words. If you cannot figure out the meaning of the words on your own, look them up in a dictionary. Note that *en* means "in" and *de* means "down from."

Computer hackers found the newspaper's website to be insufficiently protected. It took them only three hours to circumvent the primitive form of *encryption* that was set up to deter thefts and security breaches. In response to the break-in, the paper has instituted a more advanced security feature. Now attacks that were formerly *undetectable* can be anticipated and prevented.

UNIT SIX

MOR, MUR
Latin MORA "delay"

MORATORIUM (môr ə tôr´ē əm) *n.* A formal delay; a suspension
Following the uncovering of mismanaged funds, the treasurer placed a *moratorium* on any new spending.
syn: suspension

DEMURE (də myōōr´) *adj.* Modest and shy
L. de, "from" + mura = *delayed from*
Andrea gave Patrick a *demure* smile, but was too shy to answer him directly.
syn: modest   *ant:* brash

DEMUR (dē mûr´) *v.* To express unwillingness to do something; to object
Lucinda wanted to help with Rob's campaign, but she *demurred* from giving speeches.
syn: resist   *ant:* assent

TEMP
Latin TEMPUS, TEMPORIS "time"

EXTEMPORANEOUS (ek stem pər ā´ nē əs)
    adj. Done without planning; improvised
The comedian was known as an excellent *extemporaneous* speaker because of his ability to make up jokes on the spot.
syn: off-the-cuff   *ant:* rehearsed

TEMPORAL (tem´ pə rəl) *adj.* Having to do with finite time or everyday life (as
            opposed to the eternal or spiritual)
The films he directed generally deal with *temporal* themes and subjects, not unreal, fantasy situations.

TEMPORIZE (tem´ pər īz) *v.* To put off making a decision; to stall
Rather than giving the committee an answer,
the Dean of Students *temporized* until he was
able to meet with all the parties involved in the
dispute.
syn: delay   *ant:* hasten

*When the authorities TEMPORIZE, we see
John's TEMPER RISE.*

DIES
Latin DIES "day"

DIURNAL (dī ûr´ nəl) *adj.* Happening or active during the day
The new mother noticed that certain of her baby's patterns seemed to follow a
diurnal cycle.

SOJOURN (sō´ jûrn) *n.* A short stay or visit
L. sub, "under," + diurnus, "daily" = *under the daily*
The family planned a *sojourn* in Naples during the Christmas holiday.
syn: stint

ADJOURN (ə jûrn´) *v.* To formally bring to an end
L. ad, "toward," + diurnus, "daily" = *to the next day*
Because it is past the time for the counselor to *adjourn* the meeting, the audience
members are getting impatient.
syn: recess   *ant:* convene

CHRON
Greek KRONOS "time"

ANACHRONISM (ə nak´ rə niz əm) *n.* Something that seems to be out of its
proper time
G. ana, "not," + kronos = *not in time*
A horse and buggy on a highway is commonplace in Lancaster County,
Pennsylvania, but it is an *anachronism* in Chicago.

CHRONICLE (krän´ i kəl) *v.* To tell or write the history of
Nellie became a national celebrity when she *chronicled* her stay in a mental health
institution, for the country's major newspapers.

SYNCHRONOUS (sin´ krə nəs) *adj.* Happening at the same time as
G. syn, "together with," + kronos = *together with the time*
The drumbeats were *synchronous* with the band members' steps.

⚏ *When the Latin adjective meaning "daily," diurnus, came into later Romance languages, the "d" sound became a "j." This is where French got the word "jour," which appears in bon jour, ("good day") and du jour ("of the day"), and Italian got giorno, which we see in bon giorno ("good day").*

⚏ Chronobiology *is the study of the effects of time on living organisms.*

EXERCISES - UNIT SIX

Exercise I. Complete the sentence in a way that shows you understand the meaning of the italicized vocabulary word.

1.   While some desert animals are *diurnal*, most are active...

2.   To *chronicle* American history, one should begin with...

3.   Sandra saw no need to be *demure*; she felt that...

4.   The priest urged his congregation to give up *temporal* concerns such as...

5.   When asked what she had done with her allowance, Darlene *temporized* because...

6.   The governor issued a *moratorium* on the death penalty because...

7.   Chuck's *sojourn* in Alaska ended because...

8.   The play's hero is somewhat of an *anachronism* because...

9.   Lee Ann decided to *adjourn* the meeting because...

10.   When asked to say where she got the pearls, Janice *demurred* because...

11.   Rather than being *synchronous* with the eruption of the volcano, the earthquake...

12.   Nick had to provide an *extemporaneous* speech when...

Exercise II. Fill in the blank with the best word from the choices below. One word will not be used.

anachronism   temporal   moratorium   temporize   demure

1.   A(n) _____ on sales of the drug was issued so that its side effects could be studied.

2.   Verne's car was so modern that it seemed a(n) _____, especially when compared with the ancient cars driven by the other residents of the poor town.

3.   Jamie was _____ and polite around her grandparents, but bossy and rude around her friends.

4.   If there were no_____ boundaries, we could move back and forth through time.

Fill in the blank with the best word from the choices below. One word will not be used.

> demurred   temporize   chronicled   diurnal   synchronous

5. When the quiz show contestant began to _____, it became clear that she did not know the answer.

6. When offered a cup of coffee and conversation, Tim _____, saying that he could not stay and chat.

7. _____ activity in the city was busiest in the hours just before noon.

8. If the bandleader's beat is not _____ with the rhythm of the percussion section, the whole piece will be thrown off.

Fill in the blank with the best word from the choices below. One word will not be used.

> temporal   chronicle   extemporaneous   sojourn   adjourn

9. The singer said that he could not _____ the recording session until a final demo had been made.

10. Theresa's _____ poem was so skillfully constructed that it seemed like the result of weeks of study rather than only ten seconds of consideration.

11. The scribe was hired to _____ the events surrounding the origins of the royal family.

12. Holly's _____ on the island came to an end when she received an urgent summons from her boss.

Exercise III. Choose the set of words that best completes the sentence.

1. When the Surgeon General issued yet another _____ on the drug's clinical trials, it became clear that he was _____ rather than actually seeking a solution.
    A. moratorium; temporizing
    B. chronicle; sojourning
    C. anachronism; adjourning
    D. chronicle; temporizing

2. When Mr. Cassidy attempted to _____ the seminar, several participants _____ on the grounds that a final vote had not been taken.
    A. sojourn; temporized
    B. demur; adjourned
    C. adjourn; demurred
    D. temporize; demurred

3. The news anchor was supposed to _____ the past year's events, but interrupted herself for a(n) _____ speech on breaking news.
    A. moratorium; extemporaneous
    B. chronicle; extemporaneous
    C. sojourn; temporal
    D. anachronism; demure

4. During his _____ in the ancient city, Father Tim found what appeared to be a(n) _____:
   a fully functioning electric clock.
   A. sojourn; anachronism
   B. moratorium; sojourn
   C. chronicle; anachronism
   D. anachronism; moratorium

5. The _____ cycle of the lizard is _____ with the path of the sun across the sky.
   A. temporal; demure
   B. extemporaneous; synchronous
   C. diurnal; synchronous
   D. demure; extemporaneous

Exercise IV. Complete the sentence by inferring information about the italicized word from its context.

1. If Heather starts acting less *demure* at work, it may be because she...

2. If Mark is not skilled at *extemporaneous* argument, he probably should NOT take a job as...

3. Because Mr. Wong is merely *sojourning* in California, we can assume...

Exercise V. Fill in the blank with the word from the Unit that best completes the sentence, using the root we supply as a clue. Then, answer the questions that follow the paragraphs.

Riding his stationary cycle, the aging ex-outfielder looks up at the baseball game on the television screen. The pitcher for the home team strikes out the first batter of the inning; with a sigh, the ex-outfielder gets down from the cycle, grabs his bat, which has been leaning against the wall, and heads down the tunnel. Too slow to play his position in the field, and too stocky and inflexible for the demands of first or third base, this _____(CHRON) rarely sits in the dugout with his teammates, but spends his time between turns at bat inside the clubhouse, trying to keep from stiffening up. This so-called professional athlete is keeping his career alive through one of the most generous loopholes in all of sport: the designated-hitter rule.

This rule was introduced into American League play in the early 1970s, and it permits a manager to replace his weakest-hitting player in the field with someone who has better offensive abilities, but would be a liability on defense. Typically, in major league games, the person replaced is the pitcher. In college and lower levels, though, the pitcher is not necessarily the poorest hitter, so other position players are replaced. While this rule may increase offensive numbers and allow starting pitchers to last longer, it also takes much away from the game.

Concerns over the length of ballgames in the late 1960's seemed to make the rule a good idea. However, the results of the designated-hitter rule have not been beneficial. Game times have increased in American League play to over three hours on average—in no small part because of the extra time due to the offensive success of the designated hitter. Some games have even had to be _____(DIES) because they lasted too long.

National League play continues to feature shorter games and possess the symmetry of competition that is present when all players must operate under the same demands of offense and defense. Managers in the National League do have a trickier job, with more _____(TEMP) substituting for pitchers, but the added strategy adds interest to a sport often accused of being boring. These factors all call for a suspension of this rule, and an analysis of its effects on the game. At the very least, a _____(MOR) should be placed on this rule until officials know whether American League play would suffer from having all position players bat.

1.   Which of the following was a reason for creating the designated-hitter rule?
      A.   to increase offensive success
      B.   to penalize overweight outfielders
      C.   to make games last longer
      D.   to make the American League better than the National League

2.   What, according to the article, is a drawback of the designated-hitter rule?
      A.   Pitchers do not face accountability for their lack of offense.
      B.   American League games are longer than National League games.
      C.   The pitcher's mound was raised again in 1978.
      D.   There are fewer jobs for older players.

3.   Which conclusion(s) might one draw from this essay?

      I.   College pitchers tend to be better hitters than their major-league counterparts.
      II.   The baseball owners instituted the designated-hitter rule in order to make games last longer.
      III. National League managers must make more in-game decisions.

      A.   I only
      B.   II only
      C.   I and III only
      D.   I, II, and III

Exercise VI. Drawing on your knowledge of roots and words in context, read the following selection and define the *italicized* words. If you cannot figure out the meaning of the words on your own, look them up in a dictionary. Note that *pro* means "for."

When the president of the company fell ill, her husband was named president *pro tempore* until the president was able to return to work. Unfortunately, many employees were dismayed by this temporary appointment. Some were overheard referring to the man as a *chronic* liar who wouldn't even give a true answer to his doctor's questions.

UNIT SEVEN

PSYCH
Greek PSYCHE "soul, mind"

PSYCHE (sī´ kē) *n.* The mind, especially as the center of a person's being
The death of Greg's mother had a tremendously damaging effect on his *pysche*.
syn: spirit

PSYCHOSOMATIC (sī kō sō mat´ ik) *adj.* Having an effect on the body, but mental or emotional in origin
G. psyche + soma, "body" = *of mind and body*
A recent study has revealed that heartburn is often a *psychosomatic* response to the dislike of a particular food.

PSYCHOTIC (sī kät´ ik) *adj.* Having severe mental illness to the point of disconnection from reality
G. psyche + otic, "in an abnormal state" = *in an abnormal state of mind*
The local station frequently frightens its audience by warning that *psychotic* madmen are on the loose.
syn: deranged   *ant:* sane

ANIMA
Latin ANIMUS "soul, mind, life, spirit"

PUSILLANIMOUS (pyōō si lan´ ə məs) *adj.* Timid or cowardly; not brave
L. pusillus, "weak," + animus = *weak-souled*
The cartoon character, a *pusillanimous* panda, is so frightened when he meets another bear that he runs and hides.
syn: faint-hearted   *ant:* fearless

ANIMADVERSION (an ə məd vûr´ zhən) *n.* Strong criticism or blame
L. anima + ad, "toward," + versum, "turn" = *turning the mind toward (in blame)*
The *animadversions* Sam heaped on Ike at that moment had rarely been uttered by one friend to another.
syn: abuse   *ant:* praise

INANIMATE (in an´ i mət) *adj.* Without life; unmoving
L. in, "not," + anima = *not having spirit*
The students on the scavenger hunt had to collect a number of *inanimate* objects, including a curling iron and a football.
syn: insensate   *ant:* lively

▣ *In the Greek myth of Cupid and Psyche, Psyche is a beautiful maiden who captures the heart of the god of love. He comes to her in the darkness, though, and will not let her look upon his face. One night, as he is sleeping, curiosity overcomes her, and she lights a candle to have a look. A drop of wax from the candle wakes Cupid, who then punishes Psyche for snooping by breaking up with her. Psyche goes through a series of labors to win Cupid back. How do you think Psyche is symbolic of the human mind?*

SPIR
Latin SPIRARE, SPIRATUM "to breathe"

TRANSPIRE (tran spīr´) *v.* To take place; to happen
L. trans, "across," + spiratum = *breathe across*
Not even the Mayor could have foreseen the tragic events that *transpired* when a horrible storm sparked flash floods in the little canyon community.
syn: occur

CONSPIRE (kun spīr´) *v.* To plan together secretly
L. con, "together," + spiratum = *breathe together*
Candice and Holly *conspired* to plan Romena's surprise birthday party.
syn: scheme

ASPIRE (ə spīr´) *v.* To have a strong desire to get or do something
L. ad, "toward," + spiratum = *breathe towards*
Most local politicians *aspire* to be elected to state or national offices.
syn: strive   *ant:* disregard

ESPRIT (e sprē´) *n.* Liveliness; high-spiritedness
The *esprit* with which the acrobats performed their act was marvelous to watch.

In spite of the weather, fans watched the GRAND PRIX with ESPRIT.

CORD
Latin COR, CORDIS "heart"

DISCORDANT (dis kôrd´ nt) *adj.* Not agreeing or going well together
L. dis, "against" + cordis = *hearts against*
The longstanding feud between the Capulet and Montague families led to *discordant* interactions and then to full-blown street brawls.
syn: clashing   *ant:* harmonious

CONCORDANCE (kən kôr´dəns) *n.* Agreement or harmony
L. con, "together," + cordis = *hearts together*
The leaders of the U.S., England, and the USSR were in *concordance* about the plan to rebuild Europe following World War II.
syn: unity   *ant:* disagreement

▥ *Transpire once meant to "leak out, become common knowledge" (information that was transpired was literally "breathed across a wide area"). It is now more commonly used to mean "happen."*

▥ *The e beginning esprit is a sign that the word has come to us through French. Can you think of any other words that might follow the same pattern?*

EXERCISES - UNIT SEVEN

Exercise I. Complete the sentence in a way that shows you understand the meaning of the italicized vocabulary word.

1.   Alicia suspected that her teachers were *conspiring* to...

2.   Many musicians directed *animadversions* at the singer's latest album because...

3.   The soldier's extreme *psychosis* was a result of...

4.   The *discordant* jangling of the two telephones made the baby...

5.   The doctor wondered if Jill's headaches were *psychosomatic* because...

6.   Because the museum seemed to contain only *inanimate* objects...

7.   A scandal *transpired* when the opera singer...

8.   Mike's rather *pusillanimous* character was revealed when he...

9.   George *aspired* to be a pediatrician because...

10. Tim's experience at the firehouse was destructive to his *psyche* because...

11. In order to make sure everyone was in *concordance*, the boss…

12. The judges claimed the dancer's performance lacked *esprit* because…

Exercise II. Fill in the blank with the best word from the choices below. One word will not be used.

concordance   pusillanimous   aspired   psyche   transpired

1.   Experts warn that constant criticism can be damaging to the _____ of a child.

2.   Despite the general _____ between the pirates and their captain, someone was going to have to walk the plank.

3.   The events that _____ at the drive-in theater that summer night changed the young people in the town forever.

4.   Tired of being thought of as _____, Peter announced that he would challenge the strongest boy in his class to a wrestling match.

Fill in the blank with the best word from the choices below. One word will not be used.

psychosomatic   inanimate   animadversions   psychotic   conspire

5.   After heaping _____ on his young actors, the director stormed out of the auditorium.

6.   Thad's teachers noticed that he always drew _____ objects, like rocks and fire hydrants, rather than people or animals.

7.   Extreme stress, trauma, and injury pushed several of the soldiers into _____ rage.

8.   I sometimes think the weather and my job _____ to prevent me from enjoying a day at the beach.

Fill in the blank with the best word from the choices below. One word will not be used.

aspires   transpires   psychosomatic   discordant   esprit

9.   Because she _____ to be a doctor, Connie is battling her way through the extremely difficult pre-med courses.

10. The elderly musician wondered how anyone could stand a composition that brought out all the _____ elements in an orchestra.

11. The pain Kirby developed in his foot just before he was supposed to go to the dance was probably _____ in origin.

12. Learning that they would soon be reaching land, the sailors went to their posts with renewed _____ , singing and joking with one another.

Exercise III. Choose the set of words that best completes the sentence.

1.   Nothing in Ernest's _____ prepared him for the _____ he received from disgusted critics on the night his first play opened.
     A. psyche; concordances
     B. animadversion; psyches
     C. psyche; animadversions
     D. psychotic; concordances

2.   The general boomed that even the most _____ wretch among us can become a mighty hero if he or she _____ to be one.
     A. psychotic; transpires
     B. psychosomatic; conspires
     C. psychotic; aspires
     D. pusillanimous; aspires

3. The doctor fears that her patient's _____ thoughts may send him into a(n) _____ state from which he cannot return.
    A. psychosomatic; inanimate
    B. discordant; psychotic
    C. pusillanimous; discordant
    D. inanimate; psychotic

4. On one side of the argument were doctors arguing that the bulk of their clients had _____ problems rather than serious physical ailments; on the other were patients claiming the doctors _____ not to treat them.
    A. psychotic; inanimate
    B. psychosomatic; transpired
    C. inanimate; conspired
    D. psychosomatic; conspired

5. Unless something unheard of _____ before tomorrow night, Cinderella will be spending her weekend staring sadly at the _____ objects scattered in the house.
    A. conspires; psychotic
    B. transpires; inanimate
    C. aspires; discordant
    D. aspires; psychotic

Exercise IV. Complete the sentence by inferring information about the italicized word from its context.

1. Because Doctor Jacobs has diagnosed Della's cramp as *psychosomatic*, he will probably prescribe...

2. Since Buster *aspires* to be a concert trombonist, you can find him doing things like...

3. If Erica is constantly subject to *animadversions* from her family and friends, she probably feels...

Exercise V. Fill in the blank with the word from the Unit that best completes the sentence, using the root we supply as a clue. Then, answer the questions that follow the paragraphs.

Sigmund Freud, renowned psychoanalyst of the nineteenth and early twentieth centuries, revolutionized popular thinking about the _____(PSYCH). In one theory, Freud argued that childhood experiences have a great influence on personality. Specifically, he defined personality as an energy system made up of competing drives: the life drives comprise the erotic and pleasure-seeking urges, and the death drives include the aggressive and destructive forces. The way that these drives are managed throughout the stages of childhood growth and development determines the ultimate psychological makeup of the adult individual.

Freud encountered hostility for his belief that even children are sexual beings. He clarified this in his discussions of the stages—oral, anal, and sexual—through which all children go. Moreover, Freud introduced the world to the machinations of the unconscious. This domain he divided into the now-common terms of *id, ego*, and *superego*.

Freud relied on revelations from the patient's subconscious in developing diagnostic and therapeutic treatment for _____(PSYCH) or hysterical individuals. He encouraged patients to sit or lie in a relaxed position and to say whatever came to mind, thus making use of a tool called "free association" to psychoanalyze the past experiences that led to present suffering. Through such psychoanalytical therapy, Freud was able to provide understanding and, therefore, power over previously unconscious and conflicting drives that had _____ (SPIR) through life experience to cause a patient's mental problems.

Sigmund Freud's groundbreaking work *The Interpretation of Dreams*, released in 1900, also relied on understanding the unconscious mind. In this book, he proposed his theory that dreams, as emissaries of the unconscious, on the one hand represent wish fulfillment and on the other rework emotionally distressing material. Freud presented a universal language through which dreams could be understood, attributing psychological meaning and significance to _____(ANIM) objects that appear in dreams. Though *The Interpretation of Dreams* has come to be recognized as the most outstanding of Freud's many works, the notion that dreams could provide reliable psychological information was initially received with enormous skepticism in the burgeoning field of psychology.

However, as the popularity of Freud's theories grew, he gained followers. From this group emerged, among others, Alfred Adler and Carl Jung, whose theories were _____(CORD) with those of Freud. These individuals split with Freud and developed their own schools of thought, each of which expounded on Freud's original ideas of personality formation and the unconscious mind.

1. In what important way did Freud change the common view of psychology?
   A. He provided a new theory of personality and unconscious drives.
   B. He wrote *The Interpretation of Dreams*.
   C. He encouraged free association in psychoanalysis.
   D. He believed children are sexual beings.

2. Freud believed a mentally healthy person
   A. had mastery over unconscious drives.
   B. did not have dreams.
   C. had an id, ego, and superego.
   D. had good parents.

3. Why was *The Interpretation of Dreams* controversial?
   A. Patients wanted their wishes fulfilled.
   B. Alfred Adler and Carl Jung disagreed with its propositions.
   C. People at the time thought dreams were meaningless.
   D. Most people did not know how to interpret their dreams.

4. Which sentence sums up the main idea of this article?
   A. Freud invented the unconscious mind.
   B. Freud thought most people needed psychoanalysis.
   C. Freud thought most people did not need to understand the unconscious mind.
   D. Freud provided new insight into the human mind.

Exercise VI. Drawing on your knowledge of roots and words in context, read the following selection and define the *italicized* words. If you cannot figure out the meaning of the words on your own, look them up in a dictionary. Note that *in* means "into" and *re* means "again."

The sun finally broke through the clouds on Friday afternoon, *inspiriting* many people who had been stuck indoors for days. Their newfound enthusiasm prompted them to go outside and enjoy themselves. For Jimmy, the reprieve from the rain offered an opportunity to escape the terrible claustrophobia that his small, one-bedroom apartment had been giving him. He felt like a bag had been removed from his head, and he could finally *respire*.

UNIT EIGHT

CUR
Latin CURRERE, CURSUM "to run"

DISCURSIVE (dis kûr´ siv) *adj.*   Wandering from one topic to another
L. dis, "apart," + cursum = *running apart*
The professor's lack of knowledge on the subject was made clear by his *discursive* lecture this morning.
syn: rambling   *ant:* focused

CONCUR (kən kûr´) *v.* To agree in an opinion or decision
L. con, "together," + cursum = *run together*
With the multitude of opinions in Congress, it comes as no surprise that representatives cannot *concur* on a decision.
syn: affirm   *ant:* disagree

SUCCOR (suk´ ər) *n.* Badly needed help; aid
L. sub, "beneath," + cursum = *running under (in order to support)*
The crowd fleeing from the battle sought *succor* at a camp set up by earlier refugees.
syn: support   *ant:* discouragement

I offered the SUCKER SUCCOR after he lost all his money in the card game.

SEQ, SEG, SU
Latin SEQUI, SECUTUS "to follow"

OBSEQUIOUS (ob sē´ kwē əs) *adj.* Too willing to serve or obey
L. ob, "toward," + sequi = *following toward*
Journalists and commentators often criticize politicians for being overly *obsequious* to the party's leadership.
syn: servile   *ant:* disobedient

SEGUE (seg´ wā) *n.* Movement from one thing to another; transition
In my opinion, the novel suffered from the absence of a *segue* between the opening scene and the rest of the story.

ENSUE (en sōō´) *v.* To come after; to happen as a result of
L. in, "strongly," + sequi = *to strongly follow*
Flooding *ensued* shortly after the dam broke.
syn: commence   *ant:* lease

▥ Sequi *became* su *as it passed through French; you can see the same change in words like* pursuit, suitor, *and* suite. *How do all of these words relate to* "following"?

CED, CES
Latin CEDERE, CESSUM "to go, to yield"

INCESSANT (in ses´ ənt) *adj.* Going on without stopping; seemingly
never-ending
L. in, "not," + cessum = *not yielding*
The students in the class decided they had had enough of Mrs. Lyndon's *incessant*
complaining about her lack of time to prepare, so they staged a walkout.
syn: continual *ant:* intermittent

CONCEDE (kən sēd´) *v.* To admit that something is true; to give up
L. con, "strongly," + cedere = *strongly yield*
Ashley *conceded* that some kinds of pollution are unavoidable, but she remained
firm in her belief that large-scale polluters should not be entirely excused.
syn: grant *ant:* deny

INTERCEDE (in tər sēd´) *v.* To ask or plead with on behalf of another
L. inter, "between," + cedere = *go between*
Marge took advantage of the break in the argument to *intercede* for her brother.
syn: arbitrate

PET
Latin PETERE, PETITUM "to seek, to go towards"

PERPETUITY (pûr pi tōō´ i tē) *n.* A time period lasting through the ages; eternity
L. per, "through," + petere = *to go towards through (time)*
A clause in the contract guaranteed the wealthy woman's heirs access to the
island "in *perpetuity*," which made them very pleased.

PERPETUATE (pər pech´ ōō āt) *v.* To cause to continue; to further
The media's coverage of foreign wars only *perpetuates* certain mistaken ideas held
by most Americans.
syn: foster *ant:* eliminate

While we see cessum
*appear in words meaning
"to go forward" (pro-
cess, access), it can also
mean "to go" as in "to
depart, to yield." This
second meaning gives us
the English word* cease,
as well as incessant,
*which is literally "never
ceasing."*

EXERCISES - UNIT EIGHT

Exercise I. Complete the sentence in a way that shows you understand the meaning of the italicized vocabulary word.

1. Rioting in the town square *ensued* when...

2. Rather than providing *succor* to the victims of the flood, the people of the neighboring town...

3. Nothing *perpetuates* the idea of college students as spoiled and wealthy like...

4. Corey hated it when his coworkers did *obsequious* things like...

5. Because there was no *segue* between the first part of the movie and the second...

6. Pauline's lecture style was rather *discursive*, and she often...

7. The *incessant* droning of frogs in the swamp made the lost travelers...

8. The two doctors almost always *concurred* on diagnoses because...

9. Although Marlon and Amy seemed to be having a friendly conversation, Alex felt that he should *intercede* because...

10. New legislation preserves the wetlands in *perpetuity* so that...

11. William *conceded* that Annette's idea could be right when...

Exercise II. Fill in the blank with the best word from the choices below. One word will not be used.

| segue | intercede | perpetuate | concur | succor |

1. John will _____ for April if the bullying does not stop.

2. The weary travelers stopped at an inn for the night, hoping that the innkeeper would provide a bit of _____ to them.

3. The keynote speaker hoped for a smooth _____ between the debate over gender issues in the workplace and the examination of women's new role in advertising.

4. Policies based on revenge only _____ the violence that brought them about in the first place.

Fill in the blank with the best word from the choices below. One word will not be used.

perpetuity   ensue   concur   incessant   concede

5.   Bonnie assumed that the other lawyers in her firm felt as she did, so she was shocked to learn that they did not _____ with her recommendation.

6.   Nervous officials delayed the release of information about the nuclear meltdown because they feared panic would _____ once the news was broadcast.

7.   Philip's _____ giggling began to annoy the other passengers on the subway.

8.   Only after she had researched every rule on the books did Esther _____ that her sister had won their marathon chess game.

Fill in the blank with the best word from the choices below. One word will not be used.

discursive   perpetuate   obsequious   perpetuity

9.   While a(n) _____ style may not be suitable for a journalist writing on a single topic, it perfectly fits the talk show host who must cover a variety of current events.

10.   Will the curse of the vampire haunt the family through _____, or will some future heir find a way to break the spell?

11.   Vince was so _____ that he sometimes seemed more like the boss' pet than an assistant.

Exercise III. Choose the set of words that best completes the sentence.

1.   The oppressive heat, the _____ humming of an endless line of cars outside, and my uncle's voice as he wandered through another _____ story all combined to put me to sleep.
    A. obsequious; incessant
    B. discursive; obsequious
    C. incessant; discursive
    D. obsequious; discursive

2.   If someone does not _____ for me in my dispute with my family, the feud may continue into _____.
    A. intercede; perpetuity
    B. concur; segue
    C. ensue; perpetuity
    D. intercede; segue

3.   The film critic was clearly paid by the big studios, and his _____ behavior _____ his audi-
      ence's conviction that an unbiased opinion from him was now impossible to find.
      A. discursive; concurred
      B. obsequious; perpetuated
      C. incessant; conceded
      D. discursive; interceded

4.   Although Tony and I do not _____ as to what should be done on the Mortensen case, I will
      _____ that, as he says, it is too important a case to ignore.
      A. concur; concede
      B. perpetuate; concur
      C. ensue; concur
      D. concede; perpetuate

5.   When refugees in desperate need of _____ overwhelmed the camp set up by an aid agency, a
      crisis _____.
      A. perpetuity; concurred
      B. segue; ensued
      C. perpetuity; conceded
      D. succor; ensued

Exercise IV. Complete the sentence by inferring information about the italicized word from its context.

1.   Wild celebrations will probably *ensue* as a result of the home team...

2.   Because Whitney talks *incessantly*, her teachers are forced to do things like...

3.   If Marion and Chris do not *concur* on the answer to the math problem, they will probably...

**Exercise V. Fill in the blank with the word from the Unit that best completes the sentence, using the root
      we supply as a clue. Then, answer the questions that follow the paragraphs.**

Several states have successfully passed laws that completely ban smoking in public places. The strictest legislation restricts cigarette, cigar, and pipe smoking in privately-owned businesses like restaurants, nightclubs, and casinos. While the owners of these private enterprises _____(CED) that such laws are meant to safeguard citizens from the health hazards of secondhand smoke, they oppose the restrictions because they fear losing a significant amount of business. They express outrage at the fact that they have lost their democratic right to choose how to operate their own establishments. Some smokers, who contend that laws banning smoking in public places are unconstitutional and deny smokers a basic personal freedom, match the owners' outrage.

Taking a stand on this issue involves deciding whether it is more important to protect the general welfare than to protect the rights of private enterprise or individual smokers. Most people, according to polls, _____(CUR) with the government agencies' banning smoking. To quote philosopher John Stuart Mill, "The only purpose for which power can be rightfully exercised over any member of a civilized community, against his will, is to prevent harm to others."

Because research strongly suggests that secondhand smoke contributes to the increased incidence of heart disease, lung cancer, and major diseases of the respiratory system like emphysema, it is clear that legislating a prohibition on smoking in all public places has the power to prevent significant harm to all those who choose not to smoke. The ban protects the current and future health of babies and young children who have no choice about the environments in which they are placed; it protects those employed by private enterprises like bars, some of whom must otherwise endure extremely high levels of secondhand smoke. The ban also helps safeguard the health of fetuses and expectant mothers.

Another facet of this highly debated argument that has to be considered is the economic consequence of a ban on smoking in public places. The positive impact this ban could have on helping control the ever-increasing cost of health care for Americans dwarfs the _____ (CES) cry of business owners who fear a loss of profits. It also outweighs any loss of state tax revenues that may _____(SU) from a potential drop-off in business. With a ban on secondhand smoke put in place, we can help lower the incidence of smoking-induced diseases, which, in turn, will help reduce the amount of money needed to treat them. In time, we will see health insurance premiums stabilize and, perhaps, decrease.

It is far better just to protect the general public than to appease the minority who smoke and don't understand that the right to light up infringes on the public's right to live a healthy life. There is no justification to permitting smoking in public places when the result is a more unhealthy population.

1. According to the article, private business owners believe that the laws banning smoking in all public places
    A. are unfair to every citizen.
    B. rob Americans of their right to smoke wherever they want.
    C. are fine if they apply to the interiors of buildings only.
    D. infringe on their right to do business as they see fit.

2. Smokers mentioned in the essay believe that
    A. they should have the freedom to smoke in all public places.
    B. smoking is a part of the democratic process gone wrong.
    C. smoking is not dangerous to others.
    D. non-smokers don't have the right to support the ban.

3. This writer's support of a ban on smoking in public places is primarily based on
    A. the lack of any opposing argument.
    B. the belief that preventing disease is more important than protecting the income of some businesses.
    C. a firm belief in freedom and democracy.
    D. research that suggests secondhand smoke is not dangerous.

4. If people who agree with the writer of this essay were asked if they supported a bill banning the use of cell phones in cars, they would probably say that
    A. a ban should not be considered since it is up to each individual to decide if it is safe to use a cell phone when driving.
    B. a ban is a good idea, since people who use cell phones never pay attention to the road and may cause accidents.
    C. a ban like this should never be considered.
    D. a ban should be made law if the use of cell phones is linked with higher accident and injury rates.

Exercise VI. Drawing on your knowledge of roots and words in context, read the following selection and define the *italicized* words. If you cannot figure out the meaning of the words on your own, look them up in a dictionary. Note that *ante* means "before" and *con* means "with."

The Academy of Motion Picture Arts and Sciences attempts to have the *antecessors* of the acting awards present the Oscars to recipients of the opposite gender. The Academy began this practice to shift the focus of the awards from actors and their *consequent* public relations spectacles onto the nominees and past winners.

UNIT NINE

JUD
Latin JUDICIUM "judgment"

JUDICIOUS (jōō dish´ əs) *adj.* Having or showing good judgment
Kathy was *judicious* when it came to time management; as a result, she always got her work done early.
syn: wise   *ant:* imprudent

ADJUDICATE (ə jōō´ dik ēt) *v.*   To settle a dispute or argument
L. ad, "toward," + judicium = *judge towards*
A third party was called in to advise the bank, but not to *adjudicate* the dispute legally.

MOR
Latin MOS, MORIS "law, custom, habit, humor"

AMORAL (ā môr´ l) *adj.* Not concerned about morality
L. a, "no," + mores = *no moral*
Though a commonly held belief states that politicians must be *amoral* to succeed, Candidate Jeffers insists that leaders must know right and wrong above all else.

MORES (môr´ āz) *n.* Attitudes and behaviors that are so firmly fixed that they are followed like laws
Tipping a server in a restaurant is perfectly in line with American *mores*, but has no place in the customs of some other cultures.
syn: ethics

MOROSE (môr ōs´) *adj.* Gloomy, bad-tempered
L. morosus, "full of bad humor"
The overcast sky made most of the children, who had been hoping to go the beach, *morose.*
syn: sullen   *ant:* jolly

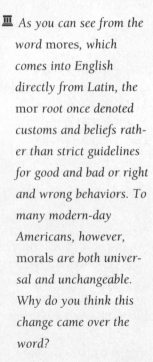

As you can see from the word mores, *which comes into English directly from Latin, the mor root once denoted customs and beliefs rather than strict guidelines for good and bad or right and wrong behaviors. To many modern-day Americans, however,* morals *are both universal and unchangeable. Why do you think this change came over the word?*

MOE was MOROSE when he couldn't find one MORE ROSE.

PI

Latin PIUS "law-abiding, pious, dutiful"
PIARE, PIATUM "atone"

EXPIATE (ek´ spē āt) *v.* To make up for doing wrong
L. ex, "strongly," + piatum = *strongly atone*
Brian offended many people during his rise to power, but *expiated* his insults by appointing some of these people to his cabinet.
syn: atone

IMPIOUS (im´ pē əs) *adj.* Lacking respect for what should be worshipped
L. in, "not," + pius = *not law-abiding*
Who would be so *impious* as to question the absolute wisdom of the Emperor?
syn: irreverent　　　　　　　*ant:* devout

SACR

Latin SACER, SACRIS "holy, sacred"

CONSECRATE (kän´ sə krāt) *v.* To set apart as holy; to give up to a purpose
L. con, "strongly," + sacer = *to make strongly holy*
The leader of the tribe *consecrated* the ground to the spirits of Earth, air, water, and fire.
syn: bless　　　　　　　*ant:* profane

EXECRABLE (eks´ ə krəbl) *adj.* Very bad; hateful
L. ex, "out of," + sacer = *out of the holy; unholy*
After one meal with my brothers, my grandmother declared she had never seen such *execrable* manners in all her life.
syn: heinous　　　　　　　*ant:* hallowed

SACROSANCT (sak´ rō sankt) *adj.* So sacred or revered as to be off-limits
L. sacer + sanctus, "blessed" = *sacred and sanctified; doubly blessed*
No political figure, living or dead, was considered *sacrosanct* by the controversial comedian.

Ⅲ *Medieval and Renaissance artists often depicted the dead Christ lying in the arms of his mother Mary. This scene is known as the* Pieta. *One of the most famous was sculpted by Michelangelo.*

EXERCISES - UNIT NINE

Exercise I. Complete the sentence in a way that shows you understand the meaning of the italicized vocabulary word.

1.   Jenny tried to *expiate* her behavior to Amy by...

2.   Our father had to *adjudicate* a dispute between my sister and me because...

3.   When the coach was greeted by seven *morose* basketball players, he knew that...

4.   The legend of the city's founder seems almost *sacrosanct* because...

5.   Do you think that all artists are *amoral*, or are they...

6.   The most *judicious* use of his allowance will bring Tommy...

7.   John's actions grew more and more *impious* as he...

8.   Even as a small boy, Ruben knew he would someday *consecrate* his life to...

9.   The only hotel that we could find was so *execrable* that...

10.   The medieval scholar compared the *mores* of his own time to...

Exercise II. Fill in the blank with the best word from the choices below. One word will not be used.

| expiate | mores | execrable | adjudicate | judicious |

1.   Libby cursed the _____ of a society that would willfully watch itself be mocked and humiliated on television.

2.   Do not agree to _____ any arguments between Kate and Alice; you'll probably end up fighting with one or both of them yourself.

3.   Mike was so angry at his sister that he declared she would never be able to _____ the wrong she had done to him.

4.   Henry's mother advised him to be _____ in his financial affairs, but still generous to those in need.

Fill in the blank with the best word from the choices below. One word will not be used.

morose   impious   amoral   execrable

5. Some advertising agencies are totally _____; they base their actions on what sells rather than what is right or wrong.

6. "Although the food was barely edible and the service _____," the reviewer wrote, "the dining room did have a charming atmosphere."

7. A stricter father would have rebuked his son for such _____ jokes and rude pranks, but Todd enjoyed his child's irreverence.

Fill in the blank with the best word from the choices below. One word will not be used.

sacrosanct   consecrated   morose   expiated

8. The battlefield where many people had given their lives was _____ in our memory.

9. Madeleine's dark, _____ expression became one of beaming joy as she realized her father had not forgotten to come to her play after all.

10. Certain texts have become _____ in the teaching of literature; anyone who dares question them is branded an enemy of art.

Exercise III. Choose the set of words that best completes the sentence.

1. Professor Lawrence not only had to make _____ decisions about how far each discussion could go, but also needed to be careful not to treat any work as out-of-reach or _____.
   A. judicious; morose
   B. impious; sacrosanct
   C. judicious; sacrosanct
   D. amoral; execrable

2. It is certainly an indictment of the _____ of our time and civilization that, in the midst of enormous wealth, anyone could live in such _____ conditions.
   A. morose; execrable
   B. mores; execrable
   C. sacrosanct; mores
   D. amoral; execrable

3. When Charles entered the courtroom to _____ the dispute, he looked optimistic; when he came out five hours later, his expression was gloomy and _____.
   A. expiate; amoral
   B. consecrate; morose
   C. adjudicate; morose
   D. expiate; judicious

4.   There were some calls to turn the train robbers' former camp into a cemetery, but Father Gwinn refused to
      _____ the ground on which wicked, _____ murderers had committed their brutal acts.
      A. adjudicate; execrable
      B. consecrate; impious
      C. expiate; amoral
      D. adjudicate; amoral

5.   Because he had a naturally _____ mind, James refused to _____ his sins until someone
      could tell him exactly why they were wrong.
      A. amoral; expiate
      B. amoral; consecrate
      C. sacrosanct; consecrate
      D. judicious; adjudicate

Exercise IV. Complete the sentence by inferring information about the italicized word from its context.

1.   If Mark's mom remarks aloud on her son's *execrable* housekeeping, we can infer that she thinks he
      should…

2.   If Kim sees Monique looking *morose*, she will probably ask Monique…

3.   Unless the shipwrecked sailors are more *judicious* in their rationing of fresh water, they will…

**Exercise V. Fill in the blank with the word from the Unit that best completes the sentence, using the root
we supply as a clue. Then, answer the questions that follow the paragraphs.**

For many citizens, the United States flag is _____ (SACR), and the burning of the flag as a statement of political protest elicits strenuous opposition. The vast majority believes that flag-burning desecrates not only the flag itself, but also the very ideal for which it stands. However, these individuals may be surprised to learn that the Supreme Court has repeatedly upheld the right to burn the flag because the act is guaranteed by the First Amendment of the Constitution as a form of free speech.
The Supreme Court has been called upon to _____ (JUD) several flag-burning cases. In each one, the Court confirmed that burning a flag within the context of a public, political protest constitutes a symbolic act. Such acts are protected speech according to the Bill of Rights, that uniquely American document which exists to ensure the freedom of expression of even unpopular ideas.

The permissibility of such expression is what distinguishes the United States from other countries where similar political protest is prohibited. In the United States, citizens are required to tolerate even the expression of seemingly sacrilegious, unpopular, or _____ (PI) ideas. Flag-burning, however, seems, to many citizens, to be beyond ordinary protest.

In its latest decision, the High Court determined that the right of citizens to freedom of speech outweighs the government's interest in protecting the flag as a symbol of unity and freedom. In fact, the Court went so far as to declare the Flag Protection Act of 1989–legislation that criminalizes flag-burning–unconstitutional.

To its credit, the Supreme Court noted that criminalizing flag-burning ignores the act's communicative impact. It is not simply an object of personal property that is being burned. The burning itself is a statement of an idea; therefore, to criminalize flag burning is to punish someone for the expression of an idea. This notion, of course, threatens the _____ (MOR) of the United States as a nation. Above all others, the one belief that binds us together as a nation is the moral imperative of individual freedom, and even the most ardent supporters of flag-protection legislation should not actively support legislation to suppress unpopular speech. American citizens must accept a challenge to their own beliefs if they are truly to adhere to the ideals of the Constitution.

1. According to the Supreme Court, flag-burning is considered what type of speech?
    A. free speech
    B. symbolic speech
    C. inappropriate speech
    D. criminal speech

2. According to the author, why do individuals burn flags?
    A. to make a statement
    B. to outrage others
    C. to see if they get arrested
    D. to gather a crowd

3. What is one reason the Supreme Court considered the Flag Protection Act unconstitutional?
    A. It recognized that flag-burning is a communicative act.
    B. It considered a flag personal property.
    C. It believes in flying the flag.
    D. It felt flag-burning was too horrible to allow.

Exercise VI. Drawing on your knowledge of roots and words in context, read the following selection and define the *italicized* words. If you cannot figure out the meaning of the words on your own, look them up in a dictionary.

Gene was polishing the vessels in the *sacristan* on Friday afternoon when he was approached by Tina, a member of the choir. She voiced her fears that the Church was shutting people out rather than providing sanctuary for them. She felt that Father Linelli, in particular, had become too *moralistic*, condemning everyone who did not conform to his rigid qualifications for salvation. Gene promised to give some thought to her concerns as he departed the Church.

UNIT TEN

ART, ERT
Latin ARS, ARTIS "art"

ARTIFICE (ärt´ ə fis) *n.* Clever trickery; deception
The actor had become so skilled at his craft that his own family could not tell
when he was using *artifice* and when he was being sincere.

ARTLESS (ärt´ ləs) *adj.* Without strategy or deceit; naïve
The chaplain's wandering sermons and *artless* friendliness earned him the ridicule of some of the older officers.

INERT (in ûrt´) *adj.* Not having power to move; slow to act
L. in, "not," + artis = *not skilled*
The desert animals lay *inert* in the afternoon
trying to conserve as much energy as possible.
syn: lifeless   *ant:* animated

Having eaten all the DESSERT, BERT was INERT.

ICON
Greek EIKON "image"

ICON (ī´ kän) *n.* An image that best represents something; a symbol
No one expected a classical pianist to become an *icon* of the new age of
technology and instant TV celebrities.

ICONOCLAST (ī kän´ ə klast) *n.* A person who attacks or mocks things most
          people believe in
G. eikon + klastein, "to break" = *image-breaker*
The television host established herself as an *iconoclast* on her very first show,
when she denounced all network television as pointless and deceptive.

ICONOGRAPHY (ī kə nog´ rə fē) *n.* The study of a group of representative
          pictures or symbols
G. eikon + graphy, "writing about, study" = *study of images*
What we know about the *iconography* of ancient Egypt is taken from the hiero-
glyphics and drawings on tombs and artifacts.

IM, EM
Latin IMITARE, IMITATUM "to mimic, to imitate"

EMULATE (em´ yōō lāt) *v.* To seek to be like; to admiringly mimic
Many actors in Hollywood strive to *emulate* their heroes.
syn: imitate

INIMITABLE (in im´ i tə bəl) *adj.* Impossible to imitate or copy
L. in, "not," + imitatum = *not able to be imitated*
The prince handled the personal criticism with his usual *inimitable* poise and grace.

VIS, VEY, VIEW
Latin VIDERE, VISUM "to see"

PURVEYOR (pər vā´ ər) *n.* One who supplies or sells
L. pro, "forth," + videre = *to see for, to see to*
Tired of his life as a corporate lawyer, Randy moved to an island in the Pacific and became a *purveyor* of tourist junk.

PROVISO (prō vi´ zō) *n.* A clause or statement that gives instructions for a potential event or situation
Included in Aunt Marilyn's will was the *proviso* that all inheritance would be denied if any of her heirs moved out of Montana.
syn: stipulation

PURVIEW (pûr´ vyōō) *n.* Range of skills or authority; capability
The receptionist said that he was sorry, but it was not in his *purview* to override his employer's orders.

Ⅲ *The amendment known as the Wilmot Proviso, attached to an 1846 bill appropriating funds for the Mexican War, stated that any territory gained by the United States from Mexico would not be open to slavery. The Proviso was never passed by the Senate, but sparked enough hostility between slave and free states to hasten the start of the Civil War.*

EXERCISES - UNIT TEN

Exercise I. Complete the sentence in a way that shows you understand the meaning of the italicized vocabulary word.

1.   Mrs. Donegal allowed the twins to play outside, but only with the *proviso* that...

2.   The newest supercomputer quickly became an *icon* of the information age by...

3.   Roger's friends thought of him as *artless* because...

4.   Katie always tried to *emulate* her older sister through...

5.   Although the singer considered herself an *iconoclast*, she was really...

6.   The *inert* figure in the doorway didn't seem likely to...

7.   As usual, Eric's *inimitable* charm made everyone else seem...

8.   The *iconography* of ancient cultures can tell researchers a lot about...

9.   The *purveyor* of pots and jewelry could often be seen...

10.   The car salesman employed a great deal of *artifice* to...

11.   Because the delicate operation was not within the *purview* of the young surgeon, she...

Exercise II. Fill in the blank with the best word from the choices below. One word will not be used.

purveyor   inimitable   artless   iconography   icon

1.   Surely, no one is so _____ as to take everything the Mayor says at face value.

2.   Was this book the key to the island people's mysterious _____, or would the strange pictures remain a puzzle for another hundred years?

3.   Although her problems were no different from anyone else's, Maria faced them with a(n) _____ dignity that set her apart from the crowd.

4.   The faded poster read, "Presenting Miss Pamela, Beloved _____ of Screen and Stage."

Fill in the blank with the best word from the choices below. One word will not be used.

artifice   proviso   inert   iconoclast   emulate

5. A little-read _____ on page 65 of the contract cut the actors out of all profits if they were ever arrested.

6. Mrs. Park was pleased when her children chose to _____ their parents rather than the violent heroes of the morning cartoons.

7. The historian wrote that every _____, no matter how radical, eventually becomes a figure to be rebelled against.

8. No amount of _____ could disguise the young man's calculating ambition.

Fill in the blank with the best word from the choices below. One word will not be used.

inert   purview   artless   purveyor

9. When Mrs. Dworsky caught sight of her husband lying _____ on the floor, she let out a shriek.

10. As I was transferred from department to department within the bank, I began to wonder if my problem lay within anyone's _____.

11. Even after winning the lottery, Sam went back to being a(n) _____ of used books and records.

Exercise III. Choose the set of words that best completes the sentence.

1. As a young man, Derek _____ the most daring and unusual artists he knew, the _____ of their day.
    A. emulated; purviews
    B. emulated; iconoclasts
    C. artlessed; inert
    D. artificed; purveyors

2. The _____ of steak knives in the infomercial always aimed her pitch at the most trusting and _____ customers.
    A. iconoclast; inert
    B. purview; artless
    C. artifice; inimitable
    D. purveyor; artless

3. With her _____ glamour and perfect timing, the singer was primed to become a glorious _____ of the jazz stage.
    A. artless; icon
    B. inimitable; icon
    C. inert; purview
    D. artless; purveyor

4.   The _____ of the ancient culture often features both running and _____ figures.
     A.   inimitable; artless
     B.   icon; inert
     C.   iconography; inert
     D.   artless; emulate

5.   A _____ in the contract stated that the city taxes would always be the _____ of the treasurer.
     A.   inert; purview
     B.   proviso; icon
     C.   icon; purveyor
     D.   proviso; purview

Exercise IV. Complete the sentence by inferring information about the italicized word from its context.

1.   If the carpenter feels that birdhouses are not within his *purview*, it may be because...

2.   People often remark that Alison's sweetness seems *artless* because...

3.   If you enjoy working as a *purveyor* of hot dogs at the fair, you are probably the kind of person who...

Exercise V. Fill in the blank with the word from the Unit that best completes the sentence, using the root we supply as a clue. Then, answer the questions that follow the paragraphs.

Born in Spain in 1881, Pablo Picasso was to become one of the most influential and innovative artists of the twentieth century. When Picasso was only fourteen, his father, a professor of drawing, handed his brushes and palette to his son, admitting that the boy had already surpassed his father's abilities. A year later, the family moved to Barcelona, where Picasso easily gained admission to a regional art school. Influenced by city life and the widespread discontent at the end of the century, Picasso broke with artistic traditions and chose radically new subject matters and styles for his painting. He became a(n) _____ (ICON) of the art world.

Picasso's statement, "I do not paint what I see; I paint what I know," expressed his new attitude towards art, exemplified in his desire to depict emotional rather than physical reality. He wanted to move beyond the Impressionist painters of the 19th century, with their focus on light and color, and believed that beauty and perfection were not the sole purpose of art. For inspiration, Picasso turned instead to the circus, as well as to the morbid side of city life. He painted acrobats and harlequins with sad, strained looks on their faces, depicted scenes in taverns and the bull ring, and captured on canvas the outcasts of the streets, blind beggars, and prostitutes. The frescoes of primitive Africa also particularly attracted him, as well as Egyptian, Pre-Hellenistic Greek, Byzantine, and early Gothic sculpture. He wished to _____ (EM) them because he saw in these styles a mysterious and dynamic force that was both beautiful and frightening. Such power continued to play a role in Picasso's works that depicted the horrors of war. Picasso often employed a woman's body to reflect his emotions. While we often see in his paintings a mother and child at peace, at other times a woman's body is literally torn apart and distorted, suggesting Picasso's anguish in a violent world.

Picasso was interested not only in different subject matter for painting, but also in different styles to illustrate his new ideas. His first masterpiece, "Les Demoiselles d'Avignon," completed in 1907, set off significant controversy. The style was radical, the nude figures were disjointed, and the faces, derived from his study of African art, were mask-like. People felt that the painting was an insult to previous aesthetic traditions, but Picasso was undaunted. He proceeded with even more radical paintings. Over the next seven years, he and his friend Georges Braque created a movement in the visual arts known as Cubism, in which a painting's subject is broken up into fragments or cubes. As with collage, it is the _____ (VIEW) of the viewer to reassemble the image into a meaningful whole. Heads could be small, with features reduced to dots and dashes, or divided in half, with two contrasting parts hinged together. While Picasso's Cubist paintings did not emphasize color, he began to use it more liberally to reinforce his themes, with strident colors emphasizing the rage of the painted figure. Picasso lived to the age of ninety-two and became an _____ (ICON) of modern art. He experimented with innumerable styles, not only questioning other people's approaches but also relentlessly criticizing his own. He brought to his canvases radically new forms, colors, and proportions, yet he believed that, above all, he was a realistic portrayer of the human condition and the tensions and contradictions that are the very essence of modern reality.

1. Which sentence below best sums up the main idea of this passage?
    A. Picasso was deeply disturbed by the horrors of war and modern life.
    B. Picasso was largely influenced by city life.
    C. Picasso was always exploring new ways to depict his ideas on canvas.
    D. Picasso was the founder of Cubism.

2. Picasso's art centered around
    A. city life and the circus.
    B. the human body.
    C. primitive art and sculpture.
    D. all of the above

3. Picasso's first masterpiece created a controversy because
    A. the figures were nude.
    B. the faces were sad.
    C. the colors were too bright.
    D. the style was too radical.

4. Picasso distorted the human body
    A. because he disliked the human form.
    B. to emphasize real emotions.
    C. to declare his preference for primitive art.
    D. because he had vision problems.

Exercixe VI. Drawing on your knowledge of roots and words in context, read the following selection and define the *italicized* words. If you cannot figure out the meaning of the words on your own, look them up in a dictionary. Note that *pre* means "before."

Felicia was so *emulous* of her best friend Nick that she was beginning to lose her own personality. She walked, talked, and dressed in a way that was foreign to her nature, and her mother began to worry. Finally, Nick himself took Felicia aside and told her everyone wanted the old Felicia back. Because he was both astute and kind, Nick *prevised* a crisis and took the gentlest means to prevent it.

UNIT ELEVEN

CURA
Latin, CURA "care"

SINECURE (sin´ ə kyōōr) *n.* A job that brings a salary or reward without requiring work; a job in name only
L. sine, "without," + cura = *without care*
The lieutenant, hoping to land a *sinecure*, was horrified to learn he would be digging ditches on the edge of the desert instead.

INCURIOUS (in kyōōr´ ē əs) *adj.* Not inclined to seek knowledge; idle
L. in, "not," + cura = *not caring*
Among the chattering, inquisitive students were a few *incurious*, bored-looking ones who were destined to fail.

PROCURE (prō kyōōr´) *v.* To get with some effort
L. pro, "for," + cura = *care for*
Even after years of petitioning, members of the small nomadic group were unable to *procure* land for the village they hoped to set up.
syn: obtain

When Basil's home remedy didn't work, he PROCURED a CURE from the doctor.

NEC
Latin NEX, NECIS "death"; NOCERE, NOCITUM "to harm, to kill"

INTERNECINE (in tər ne´ sēn) *adj.* Causing many deaths on all sides of a conflict
L. inter, "between," + necis = *deaths between*
The American Civil War was an *internecine* affair that continues to have widespread effects on national sentiment.

INNOCUOUS (i näk´ yōō əs) *adj.* Not causing harm or injury
The drug manufacturers claimed their new pain medication was *innocuous* and had no side effects.

▥ *A sinecure was originally an office in the Catholic Church that provided a salary, but did not require actual work with a congregation or parishioners. The holder of a sinecure could draw pay without care of the souls of churchgoers.*

SOL

Latin SOLARI "to comfort"

SOLACE (säl´əs) *n.* Comfort or consolation
The priest's words brought *solace* to the family in the midst of its grief.

INCONSOLABLE (in kən sōl´ ə bəl) *adj.* Very sad; unable to be comforted
L. in, "not," + con, "strongly" + solari = *not able to be comforted*
Following the death of her mother, Tiffany was so *inconsolable* that she couldn't bring herself to leave her room.

SAL

Latin SALUS "healthy, whole"

SALUBRIOUS (sə lōō´ brē əs) *adj.* Promoting good health
Recent studies have shown that a glass of wine every day may have a *salubrious* effect on an individual's cardiovascular system.
syn: wholesome   *ant:* deleterious

SALUTARY (sal´ yōō ter ē) *adj.* Having a positive or healthy result
Debates raged as to whether the tax cut would have a *salutary* effect on the national economy or whether it would force the country into recession.

SALUTATION (sal yōō tā´ shən) *n.* An act of greeting
Leonard was having a difficult time choosing between "my sweet" and "my dear" as a *salutation* in his love letter to Beatrice.

III *During the 17th and early 18th centuries, England followed a policy of* salutary neglect *towards the American colonies, allowing the inhabitants of these territories some freedom to regulate trade and govern themselves. This policy ended when the British government, forced into debt by the French and Indian War, began increasing its demand for money and goods from the Americas.*

EXERCISES - UNIT ELEVEN

Exercise I. Complete the sentence in a way that shows you understand the meaning of the italicized vocabulary word.

1.   Kyle did not notice the friendly *salutation* in Anna's letter because he...

2.   When the committee members investigating fraud discovered that Gerard was holding a *sinecure*, they...

3.   During the *internecine* period, the two countries...

4.   Being of a somewhat *incurious* mind, Robert usually...

5.   What Thomasina originally thought was an *innocuous* comment really...

6.   Though her beloved horse did not seem likely to recover from his illness, Polly took *solace* in the fact that...

7.   The mineral springs were said to have a *salubrious* effect because...

8.   We thought that Julie would be *inconsolable* about losing the swim meet, but she...

9.   Doctors believed that a warmer climate would be *salutary* for Lisa because...

10.   We were able to *procure* tickets to the baseball game only after...

Exercise II. Fill in the blank with the best word from the choices below. One word will not be used.

salubrious   procure   internecine   salutation

1.   The landmines which still littered parts of the country were a remnant of its _____ struggles.

2.   The medicine had quite a(n) _____ effect on the five patients, and they went home the next day.

3.   Before Chairman Kagani could even greet the crowd with a(n) _____, hecklers began to shout insults at him.

Fill in the blank with the best word from the choices below. One word will not be used.

solace   innocuous   procure   inconsolable

4.   The traveler asked if anyone knew where he could _____ a good meal and a bed for the night.

5.   Although the glue seemed _____ enough, it could be deadly if swallowed by a child.

6.   The support group was formed to provide _____ to relatives of car-crash victims.

Fill in the blank with the best word from the choices below. One word will not be used.

salutary   internecine   incurious   sinecure   inconsolable

7.   Maurice's puppy became so _____ when its favorite toy was taken away that it did not eat for two days.

8.   Frank, hoping to land a(n) _____ somewhere in the state government, was horrified to learn he would actually have to go to work.

9.   If the war has a(n) _____ effect on the economy, the employment rate is sure to rise.

10.   Even a masked man carrying a gun drew only _____ glances and bored shrugs in the lawless town.

Exercise III. Choose the set of words that best completes the sentence.

1.   Though Cindy's family had convinced her that sending her son Josh to camp would be _____ to his self-esteem, one look at his _____ face as she drove away made her question the whole idea.
       A.   internecine; incurious
       B.   salutary; inconsolable
       C.   innocuous; salubrious
       D.   innocuous; salutary

2.   The plastic fruit knife, which looked _____ enough and could be _____ almost anywhere, was transformed into a deadly weapon during the bank robbery.
       A.   salutary; internecine
       B.   incurious; innocuous
       C.   innocuous; procured
       D.   salubrious; procured

3.   During the _____ uprisings, almost every family lost one or more members; in a strange way, by making them depend on one another for _____, the war brought people together.
       A.   salutary; sinecure
       B.   innocuous; solace
       C.   internecine; sinecure
       D.   internecine; solace

4.   Picking up his daily stack of bills and correspondences, Bill threw a(n) _____ glance at the cheerful _____ beginning the first letter, then tossed the whole handful of mail into the trash.
       A.   innocuous; salutation
       B.   incurious; salutation
       C.   internecine; sinecure
       D.   salubrious; solace

5. Peter is so prone to disaster that it may actually be most _____ for the company to give him a _____ and keep him miles away from the workplace.
    A. internecine; solace
    B. incurious; sinecure
    C. salubrious; sinecure
    D. innocuous; solace

Exercise IV. Complete the sentence by inferring information about the italicized word from its context.

1. If Tracy tells you that she is taking *solace* in watching other happy couples, you may infer that she recently...

2. Matt is offended when offered a *sinecure*; he probably believes that...

3. In the 19th century, doctors believed a warm climate was *salubrious*; they probably often recommended that their patients...

Exercise V. Fill in the blank with the word from the Unit that best completes the sentence, using the root we supply as a clue. Then, answer the questions that follow the paragraphs.

Located in Southwest France, the city of Lourdes is renowned for its religious significance. The Shrine at Lourdes, which accommodates some three million visitors each year, is a primary destination for pilgrimages by Christians suffering from a variety of illnesses or disabilities.

In 1858, fourteen-year-old Bernadette Soubirous, who was looking for firewood, saw a series of visions depicting the Virgin Mary, each one occurring in a grotto along the banks of the Gave de Pau stream. These visions led to Bernadette's discovery of a smaller spring within the grotto. When a blind stonecutter's sight was restored after bathing in the spring, the mysterious qualities of the water were proclaimed miraculous and Bernadette's visions fell under the scrutiny of the Roman Catholic Church. By the time of her sixteenth vision of the Virgin Mary at the grotto, approximately twenty thousand pilgrims had gathered in Lourdes for prayer, _____ (SOL), and healing at the newfound spring. In all, young Bernadette reported eighteen visions of the Virgin Mary, who promoted both penitence and the _____ (SAL) properties of the waters.

Although church officials remained skeptical about the validity of the appearances (only Bernadette could see or communicate with the image), masses of believers congregated in the area. Once the visions ceased, however, a number of false visionaries plagued Lourdes. The actions of these charlatans eroded the credibility of Bernadette's claims, but she remained firm and bore both scrutiny and fanaticism with great dignity. Bernadette later went on to become a member of the Sisters of Charity at Nevers, taking final vows as a nun in 1879. Even within the shelter of the cloister, though, she was challenged by the convent superiors.

Bernadette Soubirous, who dedicated her life to religious service, succumbed to the ravages of tuberculosis at the age of thirty-five. The Roman Catholic Church canonized her posthumously in 1933—ironically, not as a visionary, but as a beacon of humility, simplicity, and piety.

Today, almost two centuries after Bernadette Soubirous walked the banks of the Gave de Pau in search of kindling, her visions of the Virgin Mary continue to inspire Christians from all over the earth, and the Shrine at Lourdes hosts thousands of pilgrims seeking the benefits of the waters revealed to Saint Bernadette.

1. Why did skeptics question the accuracy of Bernadette's visions?
    A. Even in the presence of others, only Bernadette witnessed the visions.
    B. There has never been any other claim of such a vision.
    C. The properties of the waters were studied and found to be normal.
    D. Bernadette had a reputation as a strange child with a vivid imagination.

2. After her death, why was Bernadette Soubirous canonized by the Roman Catholic Church?
    A. The Church officially recognized that Bernadette's visions were indeed correct.
    B. The Church wished to honor her for her success in attracting pilgrims to Lourdes.
    C. The Church recognized her lifelong service and humility.
    D. The Church wished to create a stronghold of believers in Lourdes.

3. What factors kept the Roman Catholic Church from fully supporting Bernadette's story of her visions, according to the article?
    A. The visions were recurrent, and, therefore, could not be deemed miraculous.
    B. The Church wished to discourage an influx of people to the area until they could substantiate her claims.
    C. According to the tenets of Christianity, women could not be visionaries.
    D. An outbreak of copycat sightings weakened Bernadette's credibility because she could offer no conclusive proof that her visions occurred.

Exercise VI. Drawing on your knowledge of roots and words in context, read the following selection and define the *italicized* words. If you cannot figure out the meaning of the words on your own, look them up in a dictionary. Note that *pre* means "before."

Star quarterback Tony "Baloney" McNair fired the opening *salvo* in a battle of words that lasted the greater part of the season. He declared that the owner of the team, along with some of the coaches, was engaging in activities that could be *nocent* to the players' well-being. He cited the owner's insistence on players' strenuous, frequent practice, starvation diets, and separation from friends and family. The coach responded to this inflammatory comment by saying, "Baloney can go fry."

UNIT TWELVE

JUG
Latin JUGUM "yoke"

SUBJUGATE (sub´ jə gāt) *v.* To bring under control; to conquer or subdue
L. sub, "under," + jugum = *under the yoke*
Under the leadership of Adolph Hitler, the German government *subjugated* a number of neighboring countries, including France, Poland, and Austria.
syn: dominate

CONJUGAL (kän´ jə gəl) *adj.* Of or related to marriage
L. con, "with," + jugum = *yoke together*
Through many years of dealing with *conjugal* disputes, the judge learned something about husbands and wives.
syn: marital

TIG, TING
Latin, TINGERE, TIGUUM "to touch"

CONTIGUOUS (kən tig´ yōō əs) *adj.* Touching on one side; sharing a border or borders
L. con, "with," + tiguus = *touched with*
North Carolina is *contiguous* with Tennessee.
syn: adjoining

CONTINGENT (kən tin´ jənt) *adj.* Possible, conditional
L. con, "with," + tingere = *touching with*
My acceptance to Harvard was *contingent* upon achievement of excellent grades during the last semester of my senior year.

To conjugate a verb is to list or recite it in its various forms. For example, to conjugate "swim," you might start by saying, "I swim, you swim, he swims." These forms are linked (jugum) together (con) by their common stem, "swim."

FRANG, FRAY

Latin, FRANGERE, FRACTUM "to break"

INFRANGIBLE (in franj´ ə bəl) *adj.* Unable to be broken or removed; inalienable
L. in, "not," + frangere = *not able to be broken*
The word of the king's minister was *infrangible* in the territories where the king held absolute power.
syn: indisputable

DEFRAY (dē frā´) *v.* To pay or supply the money for
L. de, "down," + fractum = *break down (cost)*
The senior citizens of the town wrote grant proposals to numerous organizations to help *defray* the costs associated with building a new Senior Center.

SUFFRAGE (suf´ rij) *n.* The right to vote
L. sub, "beneath," + frangere = *broken from beneath*
Susan B. Anthony was an important part of the movement for women's *suffrage*.

REFRACT (rē frakt´) *v.* To filter through a lens or medium
L. re, "back," + fractum = *to break back*
The speaker gave us a glimpse of what the war must have been like *refracted* through the understanding of a child.

⫯ *The Latin word for "right to vote," suffragium, traces its origins back to the clay tablets that were broken (frangere) into pieces for ballots.*

SECT

L. SECARE, SECTUM "to cut"

TRANSECT (trân sekt´) *v.* To divide by cutting across
L. trans, "across," + sectum = *cut across*
A glaringly bright yellow line *transected* the classroom floor, dividing one half of the class from the other.

SECTARIAN (sek târ´ ē ən) *adj.* Of or having to do with a sect; limited
Politicians made announcements on prime-time television, begging that the country not be torn apart by *sectarian* battles.
syn: narrow minded

EXERCISES - UNIT TWELVE

Exercise I. Complete the sentence in a way that shows you understand the meaning of the italicized vocabulary word.

1. Women in America lobbied for *suffrage* because...

2. The *infrangible* treaty between the countries was strained, but...

3. One major cause of *conjugal* discord is...

4. It was a relief to find a conservative politician who did not *refract* ideas through...

5. Whether Kelly goes to school today is *contingent* upon...

6. In order to *defray* the cost of the vacuum cleaner, the company...

7. The road that *transected* the town had the effect of...

8. *Sectarian* disputes within the government led to...

9. The fierce captain vowed that rather than be *subjugated* by his enemy, he would...

10. The state was *contiguous* with the ocean on one side, but on the other...

Exercise II. Fill in the blank with the best word from the choices below. One word will not be used.

     contingent   refracted   conjugal   subjugated   contiguous

1. The projected sales for this year are _____ upon the growth of the national economy.

2. Roberta and Marc cannot expect _____ harmony if neither of them is willing to contribute to the marriage.

3. The music could be described as Beethoven _____ through a disco filter.

4. The vacant lot is _____ with three other parcels of property, so leaves and twigs from the lot constantly land in these yards.

Fill in the blank with the best word from the choices below. One word will not be used.

suffrage   sectarian   infrangible   subjugate

5. Over the years, many larger countries had tried to _____ the small nation and gain its oil reserves.

6. _____ violence raged between the right-wing Star party and the more moderate Liberation Front.

7. As long as the team members continue to love and support one another, the unity of the team will remain _____.

Fill in the blank with the best word from the choices below. One word will not be used.

transected   refracted   suffrage   defray

8. After years of terrible oppression, citizens were finally given _____, and democratic elections were held.

9. The route of the first explorers was finally complete; it had _____ the entire continent.

10. After he lost his position at the software company, Bill was unable to _____ the costs of living in such an expensive city.

Exercise III. Choose the set of words that best completes the sentence.

1. The amount of money needed to _____ the costs of running the restaurant is _____ upon the market price of fresh seafood on any given day.
    A. subjugate; sectarian
    B. transect; infrangible
    C. refract; conjugal
    D. defray; contingent

2. Opponents of women's _____ claimed that voting empowerment would throw off the _____ balance that had existed between spouses for centuries.
    A. suffrage; sectarian
    B. suffrage; conjugal
    C. conjugal; contiguous
    D. defray; infrangible

3. After their successful bid to _____ their neighbors to the West, the Mongols built a road that _____ the line of villages.
    A. refract; subjugated
    B. transect; refracted
    C. subjugate; transected
    D. subjugate; refracted

4. Perhaps we could have enjoyed the article if the ideas had not obviously been _____ through a heavily _____ bias.
    A. refracted; sectarian
    B. transected; conjugal
    C. defrayed; contingent
    D. defrayed; sectarian

5. The two towns' _____ position led to an alliance between them that they swore would be _____ forever.
    A. conjugal; contingent
    B. contiguous; infrangible
    C. sectarian; contiguous
    D. contiguous; subjugated

Exercise IV. Complete the sentence by inferring information about the italicized word from its context.

1. If Ginny and Todd go to a *conjugal* counselor, they may be having problems like…

2. Jackie is a person with a heavily *sectarian* viewpoint; if she attends a debate featuring candidates from every party, she will probably…

3. If the invading tribe is unable to *subjugate* the original population of the area, the invaders will probably…

Exercise V. Fill in the blank with the word from the Unit that best completes the sentence, using the root we supply as a clue. Then, answer the questions that follow the paragraphs.

Ferdinand Magellan's (1480-1521) circumnavigation of the world began with the conviction that he could find a new route to the Spice Islands. He went to his own king to ask for funds for his proposed expedition. However, when the Portuguese court was unwilling to pay for any exploration, Magellan turned to the Spanish king, Charles I, to _____(FRAY) the costs. With the money from Spain, Magellan was able to obtain five ships and 270 men for his historic voyage.

Unfortunately, the exploration faced enormous adversities from the start. As a Portuguese explorer with a Spanish crew, Magellan found that he had to constantly force his crew to obey his commands. In order to _____(JUG) the men, he had to relieve an officer of his post, imprison some men, and even execute others. However, Magellan's unruly men were not his only difficulty. As he continued to travel, he and the crew faced many more strenuous and perilous conditions, including weather.

Two years into the journey, he found himself in a much colder environment than he was prepared for, and he was running out of provisions; Magellan's men were also very ill. The explorer realized that his men were an integral part of his voyage, and without a healthy crew, he had no chance of surviving, let alone reaching a new route to the wealth waiting in the Spice Islands. In order to preserve his crew and his mission, Magellan decided to go ashore to spend the worst of the winter in Patagonia.

Several months later, Magellan's work, beliefs, and patience were finally rewarded. Though the explorer had lost one ship and several men, he and his crew were able to navigate the difficult 38-day journey through an unknown strait that now bears Magellan's name and come through the strait into the Pacific Ocean. Magellan felt success in finding the new route to the Spice Islands was _____(TING) on crossing the Pacific. Unfortunately, the crossing he thought would take a few days actually took four months.

The explorer never made it to the Spice Islands, however, but his crew did. Magellan died in battle when he became involved in tribal warfare in the Philippines. His expedition continued without him, and it eventually reached the Spice Islands. One ship actually returned to Spain, becoming the first to have sailed across the entire world.

The human spirit thrives on learning. People want to know more about the world they live in, and Ferdinand Magellan was no exception. He was an explorer who dared to wander into the unknown and lead anyone who chose to follow.

1.   During his voyage, Magellan had difficulties with which of the following?
     A. his ship, his king, his maps
     B. his men, the Spanish king, foreign wars
     C. provisions, language barriers, funding
     D. his men, illness, weather

2.   Why did Magellan set his hopes on crossing the Pacific Ocean?
     A. He wanted to travel around the globe.
     B. He wanted all of his ships to complete the journey.
     C. He thought it was the best way to the Spice Islands.
     D. He thought they would be the first to navigate the ocean.

3.   Which of the following would be the best title for this passage?
     A. Magellan and Spices.
     B. An End to Portugese Domination.
     C. Milestones In Exploration.
     D. The Explorations of Ferinard Magellan.

4.   Which of the following was accomplished by Magellan's exploration?
     A. A new strait was revealed to his crew.
     B. Foreign wars were introduced to the Spanish.
     C. The Portuguese recognized the importance of exploration.
     D. The Spice Islands enjoyed better trade relations.

Exercise VI. Drawing on your knowledge of roots and words in context, read the following selection and define the *italicized* words. If you cannot figure out the meaning of the words on your own, look them up in a dictionary. Note that *in* means "in" and *an* means "not."

The court issued an *injunction* on the proposed raising of the speed limit of Swooper's Curve. The *anfractuous* stretch of highway, known for its sweeping views of the Pacific cliffs, has long been among the most dangerous roadways in America. Residents in neighboring towns have often complained of getting "twisted on Swooper's," referring to the high number of accidents that occur each year.

UNIT THIRTEEN

CAP, CIP
Latin CAPUT, CAPITIS "head"

CAPITULATE (kə pich´ yōō lāt) *v.* To yield; to surrender
The candidate's die-hard supporters insist that their representative did not *capitulate* under pressure, but chose to bow out of the race for the good of his country.
syn: submit

RECAPITULATE (rē kə pich´ yōō lāt) *v.* To summarize briefly
L. re, "again," + capitulum, "heading" = *to give the heading again*
The last chapter of the book *recapitulated* the major points and themes of the preceding sections.

CAPRICE (kə prēs´) *n.* Sudden change of intention; impulsiveness
The number of soldiers in the prison varied according to the *caprice* of the cruel general.
syn: whim

PRECIPITATE (prē sip´ ə tāt) *v.* To cause something to happen immediately; to speed up
L. pre, "before," + capitis = *to cause to fall headlong; to rush*
The baseball player's comments *precipitated* a riot outside the stadium.

DUC
Latin DUCERE, DUCTUM "lead"

ADDUCE (ə dōōs´) *v.* To bring forth as evidence; to use as an example
L. ad, "towards," + ducere = *lead towards*
In order to convince her mechanic that her car really had a problem, Stephanie *adduced* the fact that fluid was leaking from the exhaust pipe.
syn: present

TRADUCE (trə dōōs´) *v.* To say false things in order to harm the reputation of
L. trans, "across," + ducere = *lead across*
No matter how many times the hostile press *traduced* him, the tennis player was always a perfect gentleman.
syn: slander

SUBDUE (sub dōō´) *v.* To conquer or overcome
L. sub, "beneath," + ducere = *to lead beneath*
Security officials had to *subdue* the rowdy passenger.

▥ *The Latin word for "chapter" was capitulum, which literally meant "little head." Each chapter of a book is a small head that governs a part of the whole. To capitulate was originally to surrender according to a series of terms that had been drawn up in such chapters. However, capitulate now applies to any surrender, formal or informal.*

▥ *In early Italian, capriccio was a condition of shock or fear that caused someone's hair to stand on end like a hedgehog (caput, "head," + ericius, "hedgehog"). Through association with the Latin root for "goat" (seen in, for example, Capricorn, the goat constellation) capriccio and its descendant caprice picked up a connotation of impulsiveness and came to mean "fanciful or fitful desire."*

SERV
Latin SERVIRE, SERVITUM "to serve, to keep"

SUBSERVIENT (sub sûr´ vē ənt) *adj.* Willing to obey
L. sub, "beneath," + servire = *to serve beneath*
Although he was thought to be *subservient* to the company's president, the executive secretary made some important decisions on his own.

SERVILE (sûr´ vīl) *adj.* Like a slave; too humble
The *servile* bowing and scraping of a man who had once been a great warrior made us turn away in shame.

RESERVED (rē zûrvd´) *adj.* Keeping one's thoughts to oneself; withdrawn
L. re, "back," + servitum = *kept back*
Melora was usually very talkative, but in the company of people she disliked, she became *reserved*.

SUP, SOV, SUR
Latin SUPER, "above"

SOVEREIGN (säv´ rən) *adj.* Having the highest power or authority; ruling
When one empire declared itself *sovereign* over all the world's ports, smaller nations joined together to oppose it.

SURFEIT (sûr´ fit) *v.* To fill to excess; gorge
L. sur, "above" + faire, "to make" = *to make above (the needed amount)*
Dieticians warn people not to *surfeit* themselves on bread at the beginning of a meal.

INSUPERABLE (in sōō´ pər ə bəl) *adj.* Not able to be overcome
L. in, "not," + superare, "to overcome" = *not able to be overcome*
On the day that Dan scored the winning touchdown in the football championship, he felt he had *insuperable* strength and speed.
syn: invincible

The INSUPERABLE chef's SOUP easily won the cooking competition.

III *A sovereign was a gold coin once used in Great Britain. How do you think the coin got this name?*

EXERCISES - UNIT THIRTEEN

Exercise I. Complete the sentence in a way that shows you understand the meaning of the italicized vocabulary word.

1.   The children begging for a puppy knew their father would *capitulate* when…

2.   At the end of the news report, the anchorman *recapitulated* so that…

3.   Because Olivia decided to attend the college based on *caprice*, she…

4.   The sudden immigration of thousands of people to the country *precipitated*…

5.   The strange facts that Henry's lawyer *adduced* led the jury to…

6.   The star quarterback claimed he had been *traduced* by members of the press because…

7.   No one was able to *subdue* the angry lion because…

8.   Maria believed that her employees should be *subservient* to her, but they felt…

9.   Haydon declared that he would never behave in a *servile* manner toward an employer because…

10.   Everyone was surprised when the librarian, who had always seemed so *reserved*, began to…

11.   The queen felt strongly that it was her *sovereign* right to…

12.   Deirdre reassured her teammates that although the challenge seemed *insuperable*…

13.   Stores had a *surfeit* of books about the outrageous movie star because…

Exercise II. Fill in the blank with the best word from the choices below. One word will not be used.

capitulated   precipitated   caprice   adducing   surfeit

1.   Despite her vow never to set foot in the ballpark again, Virginia _____ when Dan pleaded with her to go with him.

2.   Tina shocked the judges by _____ the fact that her rival had a long arrest record.

3.   Never had a government made so many decisions through _____ and short-sighted strategy.

4.   Thanks to a(n) _____ of apples in a very successful farm year, the price of apple juice went down.

Fill in the blank with the best word from the choices below. One word will not be used.

       subservient   reserved   traduced   recapitulate   subdue   sovereign

5.   Because Steve knew that no one had been listening to his story, he refused to _____.

6.   The Prime Minister was _____ by his own secretary in the papers.

7.   In an attempt to _____ the rowdy crowd, the riot guards fired rubber bullets.

8.   Having been _____ to her demanding father for so many years, Alicia was unsure of what to do when she suddenly found herself free of him.

9.   Mike was the most _____ of party hosts, speaking only a few words to his guests the whole evening.

Fill in the blank with the best word from the choices below. One word will not be used.

       insuperable   sovereign   precipitated   traduced   servile

10.   Did the _____ behavior of the waiters to the master chef show their respect for him or their desire to be promoted?

11.   By the _____ power which she had inherited, the queen declared war on Spain.

12.   Even when pitted against a foe of _____ might and strength, the small band of soldiers never surrendered a battle.

13.   Harsh words between two of the guests on the talk show _____ a fight that spilled onto the street.

Exercise III. Choose the set of words that best completes the sentence.

1.   The Tigers boasted that a team even half as _____ as theirs would be impossible to _____.
    A. servile; subdue
    B. insuperable; traduce
    C. insuperable; subdue
    D. sovereign; capitulate

2.   The _____ of currency, both genuine and counterfeit, in the market _____ massive inflation.
    A. sovereign; adduced
    B. caprice; precipitated
    C. surfeit; capitulated
    D. surfeit; precipitated

3. No one ever suspected that the weakest, most _____ maid in the manor would _____ her employers in such a vicious way.
    A. subservient; adduce
    B. insuperable; subdue
    C. servile; traduce
    D. insuperable; adduce

4. In an effort to damage the witness' character, the prosecuting attorney _____ numerous instances of his indecision and _____ .
    A. adduced; caprice
    B. traduced; surfeit
    C. subdued; sovereign
    D. recapitulated; surfeit

5. Although Joe usually acted _____ towards his bossy sister Lisa, this time it was she who _____ .
    A. insuperable; subdued
    B. servile; surfeited
    C. subservient; capitulated
    D. sovereign; recapitulated

Exercise IV. Complete the sentence by inferring information about the italicized word from its context.

1. That Natalie makes decisions based on *caprice* is clear when she does things like...

2. If the crowd criticizes Steve for *precipitating* the fight, they probably think he should have...

3. If Marie is *recapitulating* a story about a warehouse fire for her friends, they may ask her questions like...

Exercise V. Fill in the blank with the word from the Unit that best completes the sentence, using the root we supply as a clue. Then, answer the questions that follow the paragraphs.

The Battle of Antietam on September 17, 1862 changed the course of the Civil War, and remains, by far, the bloodiest single-day battle in American history.

After the Second Battle of Bull Run, the Confederate Army, under the leadership of General Robert E. Lee, had gained momentum by _____(DUC) the Union Army and causing it to retreat. Lee strategized that by repositioning the Confederate Army inside Maryland, he could feed his soldiers with the food supplies there, allowing Virginians to harvest their fields to feed the army in the coming winter. Lee also calculated that his movement to Maryland would force the Union army to follow, relieving Virginia, his home state, of enemy occupation. However, as Confederate troops advanced into Maryland, Lee discovered that the people there were pro-Union and closely aligned with the citizens of Pennsylvania; they had no sympathy for the Southern cause.

Lee consequently needed to generate a new plan, and he decided to divide his troops into four sections, sending one section southwest to Harpers Ferry and repositioning the remaining units along the Catoctin and South mountain ranges.

Unfortunately for General Lee, Union Army General George McClellan had discovered the plan detailing the maneuvering tactics of the Confederate army (he found it wrapped around three cigars in an abandoned Confederate campsite). McClellan's army accordingly established itself along Antietam Creek, while Lee instructed his troops to regroup to defend their own position. By the evening of September 16, 1862, the Confederate and Union armies were in position for what would be the fiercest battle in the Civil War.

On the morning of September 17th, Union artillery initiated the fighting by firing at Confederate troops near a church. Unlike numerous previous battles in which the Confederate Army sustained heavy losses, the rebels were prepared for the Union advance and were able to repel it. However, the Union forces did not _____(CAP) under the barrage of artillery fire; McClellan's forces counterattacked, regaining some of the ground they had lost.

The battle in the surrounding area raged for over three hours and resulted in the killing and wounding of many troops from both armies. Finally, the Union line moved along a ridge, _____(CIP) the retreat of the Confederates to the outskirts of Sharpsburg and the surrender of more than 300 rebel soldiers. By that evening, Union troops had driven Lee's army back to Sharpsburg, and the next morning, Union and Confederate leaders established an informal truce. As both sides gathered their wounded and dead—12,410 men on the Confederate side and 10,700 men from the Union forces—Lee began to withdraw his army across the Potomac River.

The Battle of Antietam halted General Lee's invasion of the North and provided Lincoln the opportunity to announce the abolition of slavery in the South.

1. Which of the following was NOT a result of the Battle of Antietam?
    A. A record number of soldiers were wounded and killed.
    B. President Lincoln was able to issue the Emancipation Proclamation, abolishing slavery in the states still in rebellion against the Union.
    C. The Union army was forced to retreat to the Potomac River.
    D. General Lee's invasion of the North was stopped.

2. General Lee moved his troops into Maryland
    A. because Virginia had already harvested its crops and was unable to feed Lee's troops.
    B. because he knew that Maryland citizens would offer their assistance to the Southern cause.
    C. Because he thought that Union troops would follow, freeing Virginia from enemy occupation.
    D. to recuperate from his loss at the Second Battle of Bull Run.

3. The Union soldiers discovered General Lee's plans when
    A. they happened upon the battle blueprint at an abandoned Confederate camp.
    B. General McClellan used a Union soldier as a spy to infiltrate the Confederate camp.
    C. they followed closely behind General Lee and studied his prior movements.
    D. Confederate soldiers surrendered at Antietam.

4. Which of the following best expresses the main idea of the selection?
    A. General Lee was an incompetent leader who caused the Confederates to lose the Civil War.
    B. The Battle of Antietam was one of the most significant battles during the Civil War.
    C. General McClellan was able to win the Battle of Antietam because of his expertise in war tactics.
    D. The Battle of Antietam was insignificant despite the number of men lost in battle.

Exercise VI. Drawing on your knowledge of roots and words in context, read the following selection and define the *italicized* words. If you cannot figure out the meaning of the words on your own, look them up in a dictionary.

Children of all ages have loved the *ductile*, colorful building material known as Play–Doh. There have been numerous theories presented over the years as to where the idea for this modeling clay first originated. Among the most preposterous of these hypotheses is that a large clump of tangible dough fell *supernally*. Detractors of this "Play–Doh from the Clouds" theory claim that it's a commercial take on the Chicken Little fable.

UNIT FOURTEEN

LOC

Latin LOCUS "place"
LOCARE, LOCATUM "to locate, put, place"

LOCUS (lō′ kəs) *n.* Specific place; especially, the center of an activity or event
The lovely stretch of beach was the *locus* of the party scene in Linville.

IN LIEU OF (lōō) *adv.* In place of
The victim's family asked that money be sent to a favorite charity *in lieu of* flowers.

ALLOCATE (al′ ə kāt) *v.* To set aside for a special purpose
L. ad, "toward," + locus = *to place towards*
The volunteers were stunned to learn that tax monies *allocated* for charitable purposes had been used to pay for the new stadium.
syn: earmarked

⫟ As words entered French from Latin, they often lost consonants. In the case of lieu, a "c" dropped out, resulting in the word "lou" and then "lieu."

POS

Latin PONERE, POSITUM "to put, place"

APPOSITE (a′ pəz it) *adj.* Relevant or appropriate
L. ad, "to," + positum = *placed to*
We could always count on Joe to come up with the most *apposite* headline for an article.
syn: pertinent

INTERPOSE (in tər pōz′) *v.* To come between verbally; To insert a remark
L. inter, "between," + positum = *placed between*
When his younger brothers began boasting of the way they had fought off the wild animals all by themselves, Jeff quietly *interposed* that the older children had helped as well.

COMPOSITE (kəm päz′ it) *n.* A combination; a blend
L. com, "together," + positum = *put together*
The innovative new school was actually a *composite* of several previous educational models.
syn: mixture

TOP
Greek TOPOS "place"

UTOPIAN (yōō tō´ pē ən) *adj.* Of an ideal nature; model
G. ou, "not," + topos = *no place*
The *utopian* community Kristen described turned out to be the product of someone's get-rich-quick scheme.
syn: idealistic

DYSTOPIAN (dis tō´ pē ən) *adj.* Nightmarish; grim
G. dys, "bad" + topos = *bad place*
As the policeman told the story, he evoked images of a *dystopian* society in which everyone was at war.

TOPICAL (täp´ i kəl) *adj.* Dealing with current subject matter; relevant
The late-night talk show host filled her opening monologue with *topical* jokes.

James always stays on TOP of TOPICAL issues.

THET, THEM
Greek, THETOS "placed"
THEMA "thing placed or set"

ANATHEMA (an a´ thəm ə) *n.* Something hated or strongly avoided
G. ana, "up," + thema = *thing set up (for destruction)*
Charging patients extra fees for services they had not requested was *anathema* to the decent-hearted young doctor.

EPITHET (ep´ ə thet) *n.* A phrase or term that describes something or someone
G. epi, "upon," + thetos = *placed upon*
The teacher was fond of a particular *epithet* for Matthew, and it was not at all complimentary.

▥ *Both* theme *and* thesis *come from the Greek root meaning "to put or place." Though these two words were once almost synonymous, English speakers now generally consider* theme *the central idea of something, and* thesis *an argument that someone puts forth and defends.*

EXERCISES - UNIT FOURTEEN

Exercise I. Complete the sentence in a way that shows you understand the meaning of the italicized vocabulary word.

1.   During economic slowdowns, the general store accepted produce or poultry *in lieu of...*

2.   Before Erica could continue complaining about her boss, Lou *interposed* that...

3.   Mariah declared that doing homework was *anathema* to her because...

4.   The *locus* of activity in the mall was...

5.   The council voted to *allocate* funds to the local theater group because...

6.   The model plane was a *composite* of...

7.   Critics argued that the candidate presented a *utopian* vision rather than...

8.   When speaking about her beloved rabbit Squeaky, Hanna used the *epithet*...

9.   The judge ruled that evidence submitted by the prosecution was *apposite* to the case, so...

10.   When asked a question that was not *topical*, the speaker...

11.   Instead of finding the *dystopian* city described by previous visitors, the tourist saw...

Exercise II. Fill in the blank with the best word from the choices below. One word will not be used.

     in lieu of   apposite   topical   locus   composite

1.   In attempting to discover the _____ of the radioactive disaster, researchers found widespread damage in a five-mile radius.

2.   The drawing of the murder suspect was a(n) _____ of several sketches that had been made by witnesses.

3.   Pete sent a large charitable donation to an organization the   deceased woman had supported _____ flowers.

4.   The material in the magazine ranges from whimsical fiction to _____ articles about the current state of politics.

Fill in the blank with the best word from the choices below. One word will not be used.

interposed   apposite   allocated   utopian

5.   Though it was not the most _____ passage for Red's funeral, the story used in the eulogy made the mourners smile briefly.

6.   The designers of the music library _____ a special room for the storage of sheet music.

7.   The _____ qualities of the new civilization were soon overshadowed by more sinister forces.

Fill in the blank with the best word from the choices below. One word will not be used.

epithet   allocated   dystopian   interposed   anathema

8.   The newspaper was widely criticized for publishing an article in which a derogatory _____ was used.

9.   Greed and violence led to a nightmarish, _____ society in which no one could trust anyone else.

10.   To a third-generation farmer like Simon, the idea of a huge industrial farm tended and harvested by machines and chemicals is _____.

11.   When the prosecutor began to question the witness' sanity, the defense attorney _____ that such attacks were neither relevant nor necessary.

Exercise III. Choose the set of words that best completes the sentence.

1.   At the _____ of the protest movement, the house of a prominent doctor, all of the most _____ civil-rights issues were discussed on a nightly basis.
A.   locus; composite
B.   locus; topical
C.   anathema; dystopian
D.   composite; topical

2.   The new _____ budget, like the old ones it combines, _____ money for charitable contributions.
A.   apposite; interposes
B.   utopian; allocates
C.   composite; allocates
D.   topical; interposes

3.   The writer pessimistically predicts that many crimes currently considered _____, like murder and theft, will become perfectly acceptable in the _____ society of tomorrow.
A.   epithet; composite
B.   anathema; dystopian
C.   apposite; composite
D.   topical; in lieu of

4. _____ the boy's real name, which had long been forgotten, the sailors used an affectionate

_____.

   A. anathema; composite
   B. in lieu of; epithet
   C. in lieu of; locus
   D. utopian; epithet

Exercise IV. Complete the sentence by inferring information about the italicized word from its context.

1. If Rita brings up a few subjects that are *topical* to high-school teachers, she probably mentions things like…

2. If the new vehicle is a *composite* of a boat and a car, it probably has features including…

3. Teddy says that discrimination is *anathema* to him; he does NOT, therefore…

Exercise V. Fill in the blank with the word from the Unit that best completes the sentence, using the root we supply as a clue. Then, answer the questions that follow the paragraphs.

Amid all the fanfare about the rise of glitzy new casinos on U.S. Indian reservations, some troubling facts are overlooked. Under U.S. poverty standards, Native Americans are still the country's poorest residents and suffer from the highest unemployment rates.

The number of tribal casinos skyrocketed after Congress recognized tribes' rights to offer gambling on their reservations in 1988. Native American gambling revenues jumped from $100 million that year to $8.26 billion in 1998. The Foxwood High Stakes Bingo & Casino, operated by the Mashantucket Pequot tribe in Connecticut, is recognized as the most profitable casino in North and South America.

Though gaming has been touted as the cure for chronic social problems such as unemployment and inadequate health systems, researchers say it hasn't lived up to its billing. Unemployment rates on reservations with casinos hovered at around 54 percent between 1991 and 1997, according to a study by the Bureau of Indian Affairs, a government agency that works with the tribes.

Many of the casino jobs went to people from outside the reservation, the study found. In California, for example, 95 percent of the state's estimated 15,000 tribal casino workers are not Native Americans. At the Pine Ridge reservation in South Dakota, unemployment among the Oglala Sioux actually increased from 73 percent in 1991 to 74 percent in 1997, despite the opening of the tribe's casino. Resignation has set in among many of the Sioux, who have stopped looking for work.

Significant portions of the Indian gaming revenues are _____(LOC) to outside companies hired by the tribes to oversee casino operations, the BIA found. Investigators have probed the companies' ties to organized crime and the rise of corruption among tribal leaders amid the billions generated by legal gambling. In January 2001, for example, a judge sentenced Fred Dakota, former tribal chairman for Michigan's Keweenaw Bay tribe, to two years in prison for taking kickbacks from a slot machine company.

The failure of gaming to raise Native American people out of poverty is particularly galling given the depth of the problem. The 1990 U.S. Census found that 31 percent of the country's indigenous people live below the poverty line, meaning the average Native American earns less than $6,300 per year as an individual; a family of four earns less than $12,674. Only 13 percent of the rest of the entire U.S. population falls into this category.

Native Americans comprise 76 percent of welfare recipients in some counties in North Dakota, South Dakota, Montana, and Alaska. Activists have denounced the government and tribal councils for fostering abominable living conditions on some reservations. On one Navajo Reservation in Arizona, 54 percent of residents don't have indoor plumbing. Some elderly Sioux on the Pine Ridge Reservation have frozen to death in the harsh South Dakota winters because of inadequate housing. Residents were even found living in unheated, discarded school buses.

The answer to Native American poverty problems obviously isn't gaming alone, says Tex Hall, chairman of the National Congress of American Indians. Hall asked federal officials to urge private industry to bring 100,000 new jobs to U.S. reservations by 2010. Without more assistance from state and federal governments and the private sector, the Native American population will continue to face the scourge of poverty. The _____(TOP) promise of reservation-owned gambling cannot survive the harsh light of reality.

1. The author of this passage believes that Indian gaming is
    A. immoral.
    B. a boon to Native Americans.
    C. lifting Native Americans out of poverty.
    D. a threat to Native Americans' lives.
    E. only one component of poverty relief.

2. Which statement best sums the main idea of this passage?
    A. Gaming hasn't lived up to its billing as the cure for Native American poverty.
    B. Poverty rates among Native Americans are comparable to those of other minority groups in the U.S.
    C. Gaming is a significant economic catalyst for most reservations.
    D. Gaming alone can alleviate poverty on reservations.
    E. The mafia controls Native American gaming.

3. According to a Bureau of Indian Affairs study, reservation-based casinos in California employ
    A. an overwhelming number of Native Americans.
    B. no Native Americans.
    C. a few Native Americans.
    D. a host of Native Americans.
    E. a tiny percentage of Native Americans.

4. Gaming has generated billions of dollars that have
    A. gone exclusively to Native American tribes.
    B. lined the pockets of mobsters.
    C. raised questions about corruption among tribal leaders.
    D. lifted the Native American people out of poverty.
    E. made all the tribes rich.

5. The best title for this passage would be
    A. Gaming: "The Silver Bullet" For Native American Poverty
    B. Casinos On The Reservation: The Indian Full-Employment Act
    C. Gambling Becomes The Savior of Native Americans
    D. Gaming Found to be a Mixed Blessing for Native Americans
    E. Despite All the Hype, Gaming Promise Unfulfilled for Native Americans

Exercise VI. Drawing on your knowledge of roots and words in context, read the following selection and define the *italicized* words. If you cannot figure out the meaning of the words on your own, look them up in a dictionary. Note that *meta* means "changed" and *trans* means "across."

Although present-day English words bear some similarity to their ancient forebears, significant phonetic changes have occurred in some words. As a result of *metathesis*, for instance, the Old English "thrid" became the modern "third." Linguists have noticed that when letters are *transposed* in one word, a similar change may affect words that sound like that word. The Old English "brid," on the same pattern as "thrid," became "bird."

UNIT FIFTEEN

LOQ, LOC
Latin LOQUI, LOCUTUS "to speak"

MAGNILOQUENT (mâg nəl´ ə kwent) *adj.* High-flown and elevated in speech
L. magnus, "great, grand" + loqui = *grandly speaking*
Magniloquent speeches about victory were of little comfort to the families of soldiers far away at war.

LOQUACIOUS (lō kwā´ shəs) *adj.* Very talkative
Thanks to his *loquacious* host, Robert soon knew everything he needed to know about what was going on in the city.
syn: chatty

CIRCUMLOCUTION (sûr kəm lō kyōō shən) *n.* Roundabout or overly long way of saying something
L. circum, "around" + locutus = *speaking around*
We decided that Sarah must have been schooled in the art of *circumlocution*, since we could never get a straight answer out of her.

COLLOQUY (kə´ lə kwē) *n.* Formal conversation or dialogue
L. con, "together," + loqui = *speaking together*
The *colloquy* between the two scholars was generally good-natured, although they fundamentally disagreed upon some points.

OBLOQUY (äb´ lə kwē) *n.* Harsh criticism; abuse
L. ob, "against," + loqui = *speaking against*
The *obloquy* hurled by the teacher at her students made many of the children hate school for life.

▥ A colloquium *is a scholarly gathering at which people interested in a particular subject exchange views, findings, and expectations. For example, the political science department of a university might host a col-loquium entitled* The Impact of John F. Kennedy On Modern Politics.

When I pressed the wrong OBOE KEY, I was showered with OBLOQUY.

SIGN

Latin SIGNUM "sign"
SIGNARE, SIGNATUM "to sign"

CONSIGN (kən sīn´) *v.* To deliver, especially to a negative fate or outcome
L. con, "strongly," + signare = *to sign over*
Gerard practiced his drums obsessively because he did not want to be *consigned* to the ranks of the lesser musicians.
syn: relegate

RESIGNATION (rez´ ig nā shən) *n.* Acceptance of something that cannot be avoided; patient submission
L. re, "back," + signare, "to sign" = *to take back a signature*
Isabel boarded the bus with a sense of *resignation*, knowing there was little chance that she would arrive on time.

SIGNATORY (sig nə tōr´ ē) *n.* A party to a contract, treaty or other legal document
None of the *signatories* to the original pact was alive by the time it was supposed to pay off.

SCRIB

Latin SCRIBERE, SCRIPTUM, "to write, draw"

PROSCRIBE (prō skrīb´) *v.* To forbid; to outlaw
L. pro, "forth," + scribere = *to write forth*
Orthodox Judaism *proscribes* the consumption of pork and foods made from pork.
syn: prohibit

ASCRIBE (ə skrīb´) *v.* To think of as belonging to or coming from; to assign
L. ad, "toward," + scribere = *to write towards*
Though many people *ascribe* a sinister motive to the doctor, he was simply trying to treat his patients the best way he knew how.

CIRCUMSCRIBE (sur´ kəm skrīb) *v.* To tightly limit or restrict
L. circum, "around," + scribere = *draw around*
New, stricter rules for obtaining a driver's license will surely *circumscribe* the privileges of this year's driving-age youth.
syn: confine, restrict

To be conscripted *(con, "together," + scriptum) is to be forcibly enrolled into a military unit, or to be drafted. A person who is drafted is referred to as a* conscript.

EXERCISES - UNIT FIFTEEN

Exercise I. Complete the sentence in a way that shows you understand the meaning of the italicized vocabulary word.

1.   Margaret faced the examination with *resignation* because...

2.   Seth sometimes felt so *circumscribed* by his parents' rules that he wanted to...

3.   It was important that the town's representative be a *signatory* to the treaty because...

4.   Because Isabel's answer to the question did not amount to much more than *circumlocution*...

5.   Psychologists *ascribed* the increase in juvenile hyperactivity to...

6.   A series of major losses seemed to *consign* the volleyball team to...

7.   The principal nicknamed my sister "*Loquacious* Lucy" because she...

8.   Mr. Stanley's *magniloquent* manner of speaking was enhanced by...

9.   The Church *proscribed* contact with the group that had revolted because...

10.   Everyone agreed that *obloquy* in the office had gotten out of hand when...

11.   The *colloquy* between the two diplomats resulted in...

Exercise II. Fill in the blank with the best word from the choices below. One word will not be used.

signatories   loquacious   proscribes   colloquy   circumlocution

1.   The oath taken by all medical students as they become doctors _____ doing harm to any patient.

2.   Extended _____ between the two groups may help them reach some sort of an agreement.

3.   Many of the _____ to the current contract have died or moved away.

4.   The suspect's _____ made the police suspicious about what he was trying to hide.

Fill in the blank with the best word from the choices below. One word will not be used.

> obloquy   loquacious   ascribe   consign   resignation

5.   _____ in campaign ads reached a fever pitch as the various political candidates grew more enraged at one another.

6.   Slow sales and lack of attention may _____ the group's album to the bargain bin.

7.   No one minded that Katie was so _____ because her endless chatter was constantly amusing.

8.   The expression of _____ on Laura's face made us wonder if she had given up hope.

Fill in the blank with the best word from the choices below. One word will not be used.

> proscribed   circumscribing   magniloquent   ascribed

9.   George's extremely strict father had a hard time convincing his children he was _____ them for their own benefit.

10. Many correctable health problems that were once _____ to viral infections have now been linked to vitamin deficiencies.

11. Even the most _____ speakers found it difficult to transform such graphic and disturbing subject matter into eloquent lines of text.

Exercise III. Choose the set of words that best completes the sentence.

1.   Many terrible things have been _____ to the General, but none so vicious and untrue as to constitute _____.
     A.   consigned; colloquy
     B.   circumscribed; obloquy
     C.   ascribed; resignation
     D.   ascribed; obloquy

2.   Sandra invited her _____ neighbor in with a sense of _____, knowing she would have to spend the rest of the afternoon on the listening end of the conversation.
     A.   magniloquent; colloquy
     B.   loquacious; obloquy
     C.   loquacious; resignation
     D.   magniloquent; signatory

3.   Although he was aware that the commandments of his religion _____ lying, Ron felt that a bit of _____ would hardly cost him his soul.
     A.   circumscribed; colloquy
     B.   proscribed; circumlocution
     C.   consigned; resignation
     D.   circumscribed; resignation

4. If you _____ your creative impulses too severely, you may _____ your novel to a place beside all the other dull, sterile books that no one ever reads.
    A. proscribe; consign
    B. ascribe; colloquy
    C. circumscribe; consign
    D. consign; proscribe

5. On this grave and historic occasion, each _____ of the document felt pressed to give a more _____ speech than the last.
    A. signatory; magniloquent
    B. colloquy; loquacious
    C. obloquy; magniloquent
    D. colloquy; ascribe

Exercise IV. Complete the sentence by inferring information about the italicized word from its context.

1. At the end of a *magniloquent* speech, an audience may feel…

2. If dancing and playing cards are not *proscribed* by Laura's church, it is probably because…

3. If a major news organization is accused of promoting *obloquy*, it may have…

Exercise V. Fill in the blank with the word from the Unit that best completes the sentence, using the root we supply as a clue. Then, answer the questions that follow the paragraphs.

American politicians campaigning for federal office must be all things to all people in order to get elected and re-elected; this unwritten policy forces them to be champions of compromise and to hire competent speechwriters. A speechwriter is potentially the most important member of the campaign staff. He or she is the communication link between the politician, the media, and the voters. It is the speechwriter's job to state, in a clear and concise manner, the politician's stand on various issues confronting the nation. When every word a candidate utters is dissected by the American press, political activist groups, opponents, party members, and concerned citizens, a single misstatement can be disastrous.

However, no speech can be delivered as a confusing _____(LOQ). Most Presidents, Senators, and Representatives have college degrees, but the majority of Americans do not. A good number of politicians have been successful entrepreneurs and dealt with complicated business transactions; however, most Americans are from the working class. Therefore, the speechwriter must write in simple language for broad appeal. This is what intellectuals call "dumbing down." No voter can devote hours to reading thick documents relating to treaties, military functions, bills, foreign affairs, taxes, and trade. Citizens want the Fourth Estate to do that for them. The link from the politicians to the American voter is the speechwriter, who must summarize and translate complex political ideologies into catchy buzzwords that will appeal to the American public. With so many news agencies vying for the quick story and the sound bite, no one can afford to spend more than two minutes on even complex issues.

Whether or not you, as a voter, agree with this treatment of the American people is inconsequential; it's a fact of political campaigns. Every news conference or campaign speech is choreographed like a Broadway play. No politician ever steps to the podium without long and serious rehearsal. Tone of voice and word choice are just as important as subject matter. A _____(LOQ) presentation will likely alienate much of the audience.

Furthermore, the beliefs the speechwriter _____ (SCRIB) to the politician may simply be those of the constituency or political party; members of the staff carefully study opinion polls to determine these beliefs. It seems unlikely that things will change until politicians recognize that their constituents want more than politics currently delivers.

1.   What is the speechwriter's primary function?
     A.   to assist the candidate's election campaign
     B.   to effectively communicate the candidate's agenda to the voters
     C.   to edit all speeches before the candidate speaks
     D.   to give opinions and advice to the candidate

2.   What style of writing must the speechwriter employ in order to get the candidate's message across to the most voters?
     A.   a highly detailed technical style
     B.   a short, academic style explaining the issues of the day
     C.   a concise, simply written format for broad appeal
     D.   an angry, passionate, and rebellious style

3.   What is the role of the American press in political campaigns?
     A.   to relay the politicians' message to the general public
     B.   to interject their own personal feelings about the candidate
     C.   to find scandal
     D.   to support the politician of their choice

Exercise VI. Drawing on your knowledge of roots and words in context, read the following selection and define the *italicized* words. If you cannot figure out the meaning of the words on your own, look them up in a dictionary.

Linda and Jamal Reynolds had their whale-bone bedposts *inscribed* with a Shakespearean sonnet. They were inspired to have the bed made after hearing of similar beds at a Shakespeare for Shark-Haters *colloquium* this past fall. Linda claims the new frame allows her "soul to swim with the Bard."

UNIT SIXTEEN

VOC
Latin VOX, VOCIS "voice"
VOCARE, VOCATUM "to call"

VOCIFEROUS (vō sif´ ər əs) *adj.* Loud and noisy in making one's feelings known
L. vocis + ferre, "to bear, carry" = *with voice carrying*
The *vociferous* opponents of animal testing marched toward the cosmetics company.
syn: strident

AVOCATION (a vō kā´ shən) *n.* Something done for pleasure; hobby
L. ad, "towards," + vocatum = *called toward*
Wesley's art teacher at first pursued painting as an *avocation* rather than a serious career.

VOCATION (vō kā´ shən) *n.* Profession; trade
Sonny thought his *vocation* was in engineering, but was not sure he could survive the rigorous program at his university.
syn: occupation

UNIVOCAL (yū niv´ i kəl) *adj.* Having a single, clear meaning
L. uni, "one," + vocis = *one voice*
The astronomers' findings were *univocal*; life had been discovered on Galtron-5.

TAC
Latin TACERE, TACITUS "to be silent"

RETICENT (ret´ ə sənt) *adj.* Not saying much; tight-lipped
His family noticed that Robert had become *reticent* about expressing his feelings following his uncle's death, so they advised him to see a therapist.

TACIT (tas´it) *adj.* Understood as meant but not openly said; implied
Although the news had not been made official, the members of the faculty had a *tacit* understanding that this was the principal's last year.

TACITURN (tas´ ə turn) *adj.* Characterized by infrequent speech; silent
The story is of a mysterious, *taciturn* nobleman whose silence hides a heart of gold.
                    ant: talkative

How are we supposed to LEARN when our teacher's so TACITURN?

▥ *In addition to these vocabulary words, we get the word* vouch *from* vocare. *When French was the language of the courts in England, to* vouch *was to call someone as a witness. The person called might be asked to give evidence in support of someone's good character or standing. Vouch still carries this meaning today.*

▥ *Sandfly fever is a viral disease that affects people in warm coastal areas. It is also called* pappataci *fever; in Italian, the sandfly is the one who eats (pappare) silently (taci).*

VERB
Latin VERBUM "word"

VERBIAGE (vûr´ bē ij) *n.* An overabundance of words; excessive wordiness
Charles Dickens was so fond of *verbiage* in his books that many claimed he was
paid by the word.

VERBATIM (vûr bāt´ əm) *adj.* Word for word
The CEO was looking to find a secretary who was able to transcribe memos *verbatim* and without any errors.

VERBOSE (vûr bōs´) *adj.* Using too many words
Rev. Parlatone gave such a *verbose* sermon that his congregation prayed he would
come to the conclusion.

ant: concise

▥ *A proverb (pro, "forth," + verbum) is a short statement that has been said before, is often repeated, and expresses a universal truth.*

EXERCISES - UNIT SIXTEEN

Exercise I. Complete the sentence in a way that shows you understand the meaning of the italicized vocabulary word.

1.   The most *vociferous* supporters of the Mayor were people who...

2.   The article's confusing *verbiage* left readers wishing that...

3.   Clarence believed that his *vocation* must lie in the medical field, because he...

4.   Sylvia indicated her *tacit* agreement with Reggie by...

5.   While Will thought the message of the novel was *univocal*, Elyssa thought...

6.   When dealing with some of his more *reticent* students, Mr. Parker...

7.   Because Leonard's *avocation* was restoring old bicycles, he...

8.   Bill's first attempt at a novel was so *verbose* that...

9.   Carlos did not take down the phone message *verbatim* because...

10. My uncle was a *taciturn* man who very rarely...

Exercise II. Fill in the blank with the best word from the choices below. One word will not be used.

avocation   verbatim   verbose   tacit   univocal

1.   The meaning of the strange events of that day was far from _____.

2.   Although he had originally wished to be a professional chef, Darien eventually decided to cook only as an _____.

3.   If the instruction manual had been less _____, the company would have saved time, paper, and confusion on the part of their customers.

4.   The friends seemed to have made a _____ agreement never to speak of that terrible night to anyone.

Fill in the blank with the best word from the choices below. One word will not be used.

vociferous   vocation   taciturn   verbiage

5. During one especially _____ period, the elderly gentleman shunned conversation with any other human being for four weeks.

6. Noting the _____ protest that arose when he tried to shut down the playground, the Mayor withdrew his proposal.

7. No amount of fancy _____ could disguise the negative implications of the company's third-quarter report.

Fill in the blank with the best word from the choices below. One word will not be used.

avocation   verbatim   reticent   vocation

8. Frank's family told him he had a(n) _____ in medicine, but he wished to pursue a career in music.

9. Our overseas correspondent claims that she has transmitted the statement _____ from the top army official.

10. Although Lisa was often _____ about her true feelings, it was easy to see how she felt about the car.

Exercise III. Choose the set of words that best completes the sentence.

1. The significance of the new environmental study was _____, but researchers and government authorities had a(n) _____ arrangement not to discuss the findings.
    A. reticent; univocal
    B. verbatim; reticent
    C. univocal; tacit
    D. taciturn; verbatim

2. It was difficult to understand how such a(n) _____ and unrestrained writer could be so _____ and unapproachable in person.
    A. verbose; taciturn
    B. verbatim; reticent
    C. vociferous; verbose
    D. univocal; reticent

3. A person with an irresistible attraction to _____ may have a _____ as a writer of advertisements or tabloids.
    A. avocation; verbiage
    B. verbiage; vocation
    C. vocation; tacit
    D. avocation, vocation

4. From years of developing his _____ as an amateur mimic, Brian could now repeat any sentence _____ after hearing it only once.
    A. verbiage; tacit
    B. vocation; verbose
    C. avocation; verbatim
    D. vocation; vociferous

5. Although the suspect was _____ about his whereabouts on the night of June third, he was _____ in his demand for a lawyer.
    A. taciturn; univocal
    B. reticent; vociferous
    C. reticent; verbatim
    D. vociferous; reticent

Exercise IV. Complete the sentence by inferring information about the italicized word from its context.

1. If Bobby and Connie have a *tacit* agreement not to mention the car crash, they have probably NOT...

2. Because Hal is a *vociferous* opponent of new development in his town, he can often be seen...

3. If Gina is *reticent* about her connection to the man accused of embezzling, investigators may suspect that...

Exercise V. Fill in the blank with the word from the Unit that best completes the sentence, using the root we supply as a clue. Then, answer the questions that follow the paragraphs.

Recently, doctors and researchers have observed an increase in the incidence of autism throughout the world. Presently, no solid explanation exists for this phenomenon, but the medical community continues to study possible causes and treatments. Many researchers contend that autism is genetic, noting that parents who have one autistic child have a statistically greater chance of having another autistic child. As the population grows, therefore, so will the number of individuals affected by autism. Other researchers suggest that the disorder results from the mercury content in routine childhood vaccinations, reporting that many parents observed their children meeting normal developmental milestones prior to the vaccine, but noticed symptoms of autism shortly thereafter. Others contend that the number of autism cases has not risen along with the population, but that cases once diagnosed as mental retardation are now being correctly identified as autism. Only recently has the medical community developed proper guidelines for accurate diagnosis of this condition, which may explain the disagreements among researchers.

Clearly, researchers operate under a great degree of uncertainty concerning the causes of autism. They do, however, agree regarding the classification of the condition. People who suffer from autism exhibit permanent abnormalities in their brain structures. Those afflicted demonstrate peculiarities in social behavior and an uncompromising reliance on routine and structure, both of which usually appear before preschool. Autistic children are markedly _____(TAC) and have difficulty forming bonds with parents, caretakers, and siblings. They suffer impeded language acquisition and may not address parents as "mommy" and "daddy" because they may not recognize other people's needs and feelings. They rarely make eye contact and have difficulty functioning in mutual relationships, such as teams and friendships. In addition, autism frequently coexists with other mental disabilities, making learning an extreme challenge; children may be _____(TAC) and avoid nearly all human contact.

While the medical community can now identify and classify the symptoms of autism, it still knows very little about the causes. This mystery, combined with the wide-ranging symptoms, makes treatment difficult, but not impossible. Through intense, persistent behavioral therapy and special education, some people who suffer from autism have learned to overcome many of the disorder's challenges and have, in fact, lead fulfilling lives.

1.   Which sentence is accurate about autism, according to the essay?
      A.   With recent advances in medicine, autism is easily diagnosed and treated.
      B.   The symptoms indicative of autism usually appear after preschool.
      C.   Autism is a condition that typically affects teenagers.
      D.   Autism is a condition characterized by reticence and extreme dependence on routine.

2.   Which of the following best explains why the medical community disagrees about the rise in autism cases?
      A.   Researchers have only recently developed concise guidelines for diagnosing the disorder.
      B.   Researchers have only recently identified the disorder known as autism.
      C.   Much of what causes autism is still misunderstood.
      D.   Many people with autism have been misdiagnosed as having mental retardation.

3.   Which of the following makes treatment for autism particularly challenging?
      A.   Autism patients listen attentively and follow directions precisely.
      B.   Autism patients may experience a wide range of symptoms.
      C.   Autism patients are belligerent and refuse to follow directions.
      D.   Autism patients suffer from untreatable symptoms.

4.   What do researchers know for certain about autism?
      A.   Autism is caused by abnormalities in the brain.
      B.   Autism causes irreversible behavioral problems in all who have it.
      C.   Autism causes remarkable talents in some who have it.
      D.   Autism is always associated with mental retardation.

Exercise VI. Drawing on your knowledge of roots and words in context, read the following selection and define the *italicized* words. If you cannot figure out the meaning of the words on your own, look them up in a dictionary. Note that *in* means "in."

Seamus' performance as Macbeth lacked the *verve* he had brought to the stage in previous roles. The deadness of his performance was most evident during the crucial scene in which Macbeth tries his hand at *invoking* the aid of the witches. Seamus' locution during this crucial monologue was monotone and unemotional. Many in the audience left the show feeling unfulfilled.

UNIT SEVENTEEN

OP
Greek OPSIS "view"

SYNOPSIS (si näp´ sis) *n.* A short outline or review of main points
G. syn, "together," + opsis = *view together; overall view*
The events the book describes would be easier to understand if the author had included a *synopsis* at the end of each chapter.
syn: summary

MYOPIC (mī äp´ ik) *adj.* Nearsighted; lacking vision or foresight
G. muein, "to close one's eyes," + opsis = *to shut one's eyes to*
The administration's *myopic* strategy in this case may cause serious problems later on.

UMBR
Latin UMBRA "shadow, shade"

ADUMBRATE (a´ dum brāt) *v.* To briefly outline or describe
L. ad, "toward," + umbra = *to shade, to fill in*
During the question-and-answer session this afternoon, the weatherman will *adumbrate* the probability of severe storms in the area.

UMBRAGE (um´ brij) *n.* Anger caused by an insult or slight
Although the interviewer's question could certainly be interpreted as insulting, the actress did not take *umbrage*.
syn: offense

The superstitious man took UMBRAGE when the
UMBRELLA was opened inside.

Ⅲ Presbyopia (*presbys, "old," + opsis*) *is the scientific name for the nearsightedness that comes with old age.*

CERN, CRET
Latin CERNERE, CRETUM "to discern, to recognize, to see"

DISCERN (di sûrn´) *v.* To see or make out clearly; recognize
L. dis, "apart," + cernere = *to see apart*
Even when Meg said she was happy with a third-place ribbon, her brother could *discern* some hint of disappointment in her expression.
syn: perceive

DISCRETION (di skresh´ ən) *n.* Carefulness in what one says or does; prudence
L. dis, "apart," + cretum = *seen apart*
Travelers were warned to use *discretion* when driving through areas still occupied by rebels.

DISCRETE (di skrēt´) *adj.* Separate; distinct
L. dis, "apart," + cretum = *seen apart*
When the substance was broken down into its *discrete* components, it was discovered to contain two radioactive elements.

PRIS
Latin PREHENDERE, PREHENSUM "to grasp, to understand"

APPRISE (ə prīz´) *v.* To make aware of; to notify
L. ad, "toward," + prehensum = *grasped towards*
Having *apprised* the supervising physician of the emergency, the nurse ran to get supplies.
syn: inform

COMPRISE (kəm prīz´) *v.* To consist of; to contain
L. com, "together," + prehensum = *to grasp together*
The Johnstowne Baseball League *comprised* teams from six different counties.

REPREHENSIBLE (re prē hen´ sib əl) *adj.* Deserving condemnation; terribly wrong
L. re, "again," + prehendere = *to seize again*
The treasurer's actions were so *reprehensible* in the eyes of the city council that she was released from her position immediately.
syn: blameworthy

▥ Discrete *means "occur-ring in separate parts or pieces"*; discreet *means "quiet or secret." A per-son might separate the gold into* discrete *blocks and also be* discreet *about stealing it from the bank.*

EXERCISES - UNIT SEVENTEEN

Exercise I. Complete the sentence in a way that shows you understand the meaning of the italicized vocabulary word.

1. The Musical Honor Society at Libner High *comprises* members of the orchestra as well as…

2. Some of Mr. Lewis' *myopic* financial strategies resulted in…

3. The leader of the small band of rebel soldiers *adumbrated* his plans to…

4. The War Crimes Tribunal called the general's deeds *reprehensible* because…

5. It was difficult for Megan to *discern* Li's true reason for being upset because…

6. At the press conference immediately following the earthquake, the Mayor *apprised* local citizens that…

7. The meteor broke apart into four *discrete* pieces when…

8. Lisa was forced to use extreme *discretion* when working on the case because…

9. A *synopsis* of the opera was provided so that…

10. Patty often takes *umbrage* at her supervisor's remarks because…

Exercise II. Fill in the blank with the best word from the choices below. One word will not be used.

> reprehensible   synopsis   umbrage   discrete

1. Although the judges' remarks were highly critical, the young gymnast took no _____ at them.

2. Divided into _____ blocks, the city looked like a patchwork quilt.

3. The police chief requested a full _____ of the new legislation from his deputy.

Fill in the blank with the best word from the choices below. One word will not be used.

> discretion   comprised   myopic   adumbrated

4. You can depend on your own _____ when deciding which streets to take after dark.

5. In an effort not to be _____, the company evaluated both the long-term and short-term effects of its plan.

6. Because Coach Seville had not _____ his strategy for the team, both managers and players remained in the dark up to the opening game.

Fill in the blank with the best word from the choices below. One word will not be used.

comprised   discern   reprehensible   apprised   adumbrate

7. Because she did not _____ the risk in lending her sister money, Kathy foolishly wrote out a check.

8. The chain of islands _____ six independent countries and one colony.

9. An officer standing by the washed-out bridge _____ motorists of the emergency situation.

10. What could be more _____ than Brutus' betrayal of a man who trusts him?

Exercise III. Choose the set of words that best completes the sentence.

1. Because the loan officer did not _____ the special benefits offered by the bank, potential customers could not _____ any reason to open an account.
   A. comprise; apprise
   B. adumbrate; discern
   C. comprise; adumbrate
   D. discern; comprise

2. When Stephen called Miranda's considerate, loving gesture _____, she immediately took _____.
   A. discrete; synopsis
   B. myopic; synopsis
   C. myopic; discretion
   D. reprehensible; umbrage

3. Listeners to the political radio program should use their _____ when deciding how much of the host's weekly _____ to believe.
   A. discretion; umbrage
   B. discretion; synopsis
   C. myopic; umbrage
   D. discretion; reprehensible

4. The spectrum of natural light _____ seven _____ shades of color.
   A. comprises; discrete
   B. apprises; myopic
   C. adumbrates; myopic
   D. discerns; reprehensible

5. When accountants _____ Tom of the fact that his investment strategy was rather _____, he shot back that no one could predict the future.
   A. comprised; myopic
   B. adumbrated; discrete
   C. apprised; myopic
   D. discerned; discrete

Exercise IV. Complete the sentence by inferring information about the italicized word from its context.

1. If Barbara is critical of Franklin for being *myopic* about their relationship, she probably wishes he would...

2. If Quincey takes *umbrage* at a remark made by his professor, his expression is probably one of...

3. Because Noah has used little *discretion* in deciding how to spend his money at the fair, he may find that...

Exercise V. Fill in the blank with the word from the Unit that best completes the sentence, using the root we supply as a clue. Then, answer the questions that follow the paragraphs.

The study of literature is the greatest academic endeavor that high school students can pursue, and if students today would increase the amount of literature they read and critique, they would enjoy immeasurable benefits both in and out of the classroom. Many classes teach skills that cross into other subject matters. The study of mathematics may help a student in the area of music. Understanding the historical ramifications of the United States Constitution may shed light on current political events. However, only a literature class will teach students to think critically for themselves through the analysis and critique of an author's creative work. These critical thinking skills can then be useful in any other academic effort.

The common student lament that the study of literature is not applicable to current world issues is a bit_____ (OP). Universal themes such as love, religion, good and evil, power, family, coming-of-age, and personal quests are found in many literary forms and provide the basis for our understanding of human existence. Understanding literature allows students to _____(CERN) the questions that have plagued humankind for centuries. Reviewing an author's take on such questions provides some insights for students into how to answer these questions for themselves.

Reading, reviewing, and relating to literature forces students to evaluate new ideas, develop opinions on similar issues, and open their minds to new ways of thinking. Literature is one subject that allows students to agree, disagree, and even argue with its truths and values.

Studying literature will not guarantee an increase in SAT scores. It will probably not give a student an edge in a job interview. It will not make a student a more popular person. Studying literature will, however, expose a student to the thoughts and feelings of other human beings, which, in turn, will help foster the development of a personal belief system.

Finally, through reading the truly great literary works, a student enters a group that shares a common base of knowledge. This group _____(PRIS) individuals from all over the world who have experienced the same exposure to an author's work. This common experience does more than provide a conversational topic; it provides a thread that helps keep the fabric of our society tightly woven. It is through shared experiences, like literature, that people learn to relate to each other.

1. According to the essay, literature is the most important academic subject because
    A. most students enjoy it.
    B. it provides financial benefits to students.
    C. it benefits students both in and out of the classroom.
    D. it can directly affect a student's chance to gain admission to a competitive college.

2. Which of the following is NOT a benefit of reading, reviewing, and relating to literature?
    A. Literature forces students to evaluate new ideas.
    B. Literature helps students develop opinions on similar issues.
    C. Literature encourages students to question scientific truths such as the law of gravity.
    D. Literature necessitates that students open their minds to other trains of thought.

3. The author compares the shared experience of reading a literary work to
    A. a drop of water in an ocean.
    B. a rose in a field of tulips.
    C. a thread in a piece of fabric.
    D. a star in the night sky.

4. According to the author, the study of literature will benefit a student by
    A. increasing standardized test scores.
    B. increasing the student's popularity.
    C. better preparing a student for finding a job.
    D. developing the student's own belief system.

Exercise VI. Drawing on your knowledge of roots and words in context, read the following selection and define the *italicized* words. If you cannot figure out the meaning of the words on your own, look them up in a dictionary. Note that *thanatos* means "death" and *ap,* from *ad,* means "toward."

Nineteenth-century poet and philosopher William Cullen Bryant penned his *Thanatopsis* in response to his own doubts about mortality. The poem offers insight into one of the most *apprehensive* thinkers of the Romantic era. Bryant's peers referred to the poet as having "a big head, but a small mouth." Nevertheless, Bryant's work remains among the most important of the pre-modern literary era.

UNIT EIGHTEEN

DUR
Latin DURUS "hard"

DOUR (dow´ ər; dôr) *adj.* Gloomy and stern
Grandfather's habitually *dour* expression made my baby sister cry.
syn: sullen

OBDURATE (äb´ dər ət) *adj.* Wickedly stubborn; obstinate
L. ob, "toward, in the way of" + durus = *hard toward*
The general's *obdurate* insistence that no political prisoners had been abused was taken as further proof of his corruption.

DURESS (dōōr es´) *n.* The use of force or threats to make someone act
The witness claimed that, alone and under *duress*, she falsified and invented the information that she gave to police.
syn: coercion

FLU, FLUX
Latin FLUERE, FLUCTUS "flow"
FLUX, FLUCTIS "flow"

FLUX (fluks) *n.* Continuous change; instability
The country's economy will remain in a state of *flux* until tariffs and trade rates are stabilized.

INFLUX (in´ fluks) *n.* A massive movement into
L. in, "into," + flux = *flowing into*
The Congress of the European Union has had a difficult time dealing with the *influx* of immigrants from Eastern Europe and the Middle East.
syn: inrush   *ant:* outpouring

CONFLUENCE (kän´ flōō əns) *n.* A meeting of two or more people, events, or circumstances; merging
L. con, "together," + fluere = *flowing together*
The *confluence* of fortunate circumstances—good weather, light traffic, and a uniformly good mood on the part of the attendees—made for a nearly perfect picnic.

PRIM, PRESS
Latin PRIMERE, PRESSUM "press, push"

IRREPRESSIBLE (i rē pres´ ə bəl) *adj.* Impossible to hold back or control
L. in, "not," + re, "back," + pressum = *not able to be pushed back*
The *irrepressible* crowd broke through the doors of the concert arena.
syn: uncontainable

> **III** *Your* dura mater *is the tough lining that protects your brain and spinal cord. The name literally means "tough mother," and is a translation of an Arabic phrase meaning the same thing. Medieval Arabic doctors believed that this lining was the source, or "mother," of all other linings in the body.*

SUPPRESS (sə pres´)   *v.* To put down by force
L. sub, "under," + pressum = *to push under*
President Kennedy called upon the National Guard to *suppress* the demonstration denying schoolchildren access to classes in Mississippi.
syn: quash

REPRIMAND (rep´ rə mând) *n.* A harsh or formal scolding
L. re, "back," + primere = *a pushing back*
The college dean delivered a strict *reprimand* to the group of students involved in last week's food fight in the cafeteria.
ant: praise

PLIC
Latin PLICARE, PLICATUM "to fold"
PLEX, PLECIS "fold"

IMPLICATE (im´ pli kāt) *v.* To show that someone has a connection with a crime
L. in, "into," + plicatum = *folded into*
The discovery of Jane's hair in the back seat of the car *implicated* her in the murder.
ant: exonerate

EXPLICATE (eks´ pli kāt) *v.* To systematically explain or outline
L. ex. "out of," + plicatum = *folded out of; unfolded*
During our first class, Professor Noel *explicated* a sonnet for us, analyzing each part and then the whole poem.

DUPLICITOUS (dōō plis´ ə təs) *adj.* Intentionally misleading; deceptive
L. duplex, "twofold"
Wally's *duplicitous* behavior lost him the trust of the entire team.
syn: devious

INEXPLICABLE (in eks´ plick ə bəl) *adj.* Impossible to explain or understand
L. in, "not," + ex, "out of," + plicare = *not able to be unfolded*
During the last lap of the race, the jockey made the *inexplicable* decision to slow the horse down.
ant: clarify

COMPLICITY (kəm plis´ i tē) *n.* Involvement in
     something wrong or unlawful
L. com, "together," + plicare = *folded with*
The author has written several intriguing articles exposing corporate *complicity* in environmental crimes.

COMPLICITY in a crime makes you an ACCOMPLICE.

▥ *The skin on your face is now popularly called your complexion (com, "together," + plex). Complexion originally referred, however, to your physical and mental makeup, the way your "humors" (substances that medieval scientists believed governed mood and health) were balanced or folded together.*

EXERCISES - UNIT EIGHTEEN

Exercise I. Complete the sentence in a way that shows you understand the meaning of the italicized vocabulary word.

1.   The witness was under no *duress* when he signed the confession; rather, he...

2.   With her family in such a state of *flux*, Linda felt it would be unwise to...

3.   An *influx* of tourists in the little beach town led to...

4.   The *confluence* of the two cultures resulted in...

5.   Drake was able to *suppress* his anger about the hockey match only because...

6.   Members of the crime syndicate acted in *complicity* with...

7.   The nurse's constantly *dour* expression gave her a reputation as...

8.   Chris' *irrepressible* wit sometimes had the effect of...

9.   The Chief *reprimanded* the firefighters-in-training for...

10.   Sandra was not *implicated* in the bank robbery because...

11.   Before signing the form, Tess asked her lawyer to *explicate* it because...

12.   *Duplicitous* speech on the part of a company representative led to...

13.   An *inexplicable* increase in umbrella sales made the shopkeeper...

14.   Gabe's *obdurate* insistence on selling the car resulted in...

Exercise II. Fill in the blank with the best word from the choices below. One word will not be used.

dour   confluence   complicity   duress   influx   irrepressible

1.   Reports of a UFO sighting in the store's parking lot led to a(n) _____ of visitors in the area.

2.   A(n) _____ of cultures in the border town has resulted in a new society that draws on a blend of traditions.

3.   Laws against torture dispute the idea that suspects will only give truthful information under _____.

4.   The Puritans were not all _____, miserable workhorses, despite the image of them conveyed by textbooks.

5.   Were the men seen leaving the store together in _____ with the burglars who showed up later that night?

Fill in the blank with the best word from the choices below. One word will not be used.

obdurate   flux   irrepressible   explicate   duplicitous   implicate

6.   Because of the dispute over zoning laws, plans for the new zoo remain in _____.

7.   To _____ a novel often requires more time than the reading of the novel.

8.   Stan's _____ behavior has no place in an organization built on trust and loyalty.

9.   Delighted by Georgia's _____ energy, the casting director assigned her the starring role.

10.   Mr. Hill's _____ insistence on absolute obedience from his employees led several of them to file complaints against him.

Fill in the blank with the best word from the choices below. One word will not be used.

suppress   reprimand   confluence   implicate   inexplicable

11.   Shocked by her teacher's harsh _____, Amanda ran from the room in tears.

12.   Mr. Summers was relieved to learn that the investigation did not _____ any of his employees in the financial scandal.

13.   Debbie made the _____ decision to change key mid-song, leaving her backup singers bewildered and out-of-tune.

14.   Mariela could not _____ a smile when she saw her little brother's excitement.

Exercise III. Choose the set of words that best completes the sentence.

1.   Hearing such infectious music, even a person as _____ as Harry could not _____ the urge to dance.
      A. inexplicable; suppress
      B. obdurate; implicate
      C. duplicitous; reprimand
      D. dour; suppress

2.   Although eyewitness accounts originally _____ several teenagers in the accident, the information was invalidated because the witnesses were under _____.
      A. implicated; duress
      B. suppressed; reprimand
      C. implicated; confluence
      D. suppressed; complicity

3. Analysts can only attribute this _____ upturn in the economy to a _____ of mysterious factors.
   A. duress; reprimand
   B. suppressed; confluence
   C. inexplicable; confluence
   D. obdurate; reprimand

4. The Senator wondered why he was any more deserving of a(n)_____ than the next _____ politician.
   A. confluence; dour
   B. reprimand; duplicitous
   C. duress; duplicitous
   D. reprimand; inexplicable

5. Judging by his _____ hard-heartedness in the past, Jamie is not ready to handle the constant emotional _____ of a serious relationship.
   A. obdurate; flux
   B. inexplicable; duress
   C. dour; confluence
   D. duplicitous; flux

Exercise IV. Complete the sentence by inferring information about the italicized word from its context.

1. If Toshiro's decision to move to Chicago is *inexplicable* to his friends, it may be because they...

2. The garage owner's *dour* disposition is truly evident when he does things like...

3. An *influx* of wildlife into a populated area may be a result of...

Exercise V. Fill in the blank with the word from the Unit that best completes the sentence, using the root we supply as a clue. Then, answer the questions that follow the paragraphs.

Corporal punishment has existed as long as people have had social interactions. At its most primitive level, corporal punishment is individual; it is used by one person to _____ (PRESS) the actions (or even the existence) of another. In an unstructured society, a society that is in a state of _____(FLU), or a(n) _____(PRESS) society, corporal punishment may be quite widespread because it is direct, quick, and cheap. In early societies, corporal punishment was the norm; penalties such as cutting off the hand of a person who had robbed or stolen were common.

Corporal punishment is also quite common in individual relationships. One sibling hits another, a parent spanks instead of giving a _____(PRIM), or a drill sergeant punches a soldier instead of ordering detention. Corporal punishment is often tolerated in complex societies if it is administered immediately, limited in scope so no permanent injury is inflicted, and incident-related rather than part of a pattern of behavior or abuse. However, corporal punishment can carry heavy negative connotations in these societies.

This is chiefly because, in modern societies, corporal punishment has little remedial value. The _____ (FLU) of these factors has caused most modern societies and people to disapprove of corporal punishment, and many school systems and other social institutions ban its use. People who use corporal punishment in an educational or work setting may be subject to penalties including job loss and criminal charges. In many legal systems, including that of the United States, the use of corporal punishment is strictly limited, with excessive physical punishment outlawed as abuse. People who are subjected to corporal punishment are often protected by the law, and they can appeal to the police or social service agencies for assistance.

1. Many primitive societies
   A. banned the use of corporal punishment.
   B. had full jails and turned to corporal punishment as a backup.
   C. practiced corporal punishment in numerous situations.
   D. allowed social service agencies to help people who had been beaten.

2. Which statement best summarizes the status of teachers and corporal punishment as explained in the article?
   A. Teachers can't put students in jail, so they use corporal punishment.
   B. In many societies, teachers can be disciplined or even fired if they use corporal punishment on their students.
   C. All teachers are against capital punishment, which is the most extreme form of corporal punishment.
   D. Teachers frequently try to educate students about the evils of corporal punishment.

3. In an unsettled society, corporal punishment
   A. is strictly outlawed.
   B. is often tolerated because it is cheap and quick.
   C. shows that the government is not in control of the people.
   D. is a form of entertainment.

Exercise VI. Drawing on your knowledge of roots and words in context, read the following selection and define the *italicized* words. If you cannot figure out the meaning of the words on your own, look them up in a dictionary. Note that *soli* means "earth, soil," and *thermo* means "heat."

Solifluction in the Arctic zone has taken place over a period of about ten years. During this period, ecological and climate changes have also affected the transported earth and plant material. Certain microorganisms that had millions of years to develop strong immunity to external change have moved along with the soil to lower-altitude areas. Though the temperature in these areas may be only a fraction of a degree higher, the single-celled life forms have much more opportunity to breed and thrive. Their protection against cold also guards them against extreme heat; laboratory tests have proved them *thermoduric*.

UNIT NINETEEN

LUD
Latin LUDUS "game, play"

LUDICROUS (lōō´ di krəs) *adj.* So unbelievable as to seem ridiculous
The superintendent's claim that all schools had made huge improvements began to seem *ludicrous* when lower test scores started rolling in.
syn: absurd

Someone who alludes to something plays toward it or hints at it without mentioning it directly.

ALLUDE (ə lōōd´) *v.* To mention without going into detail
L. ad, "toward," + ludus = *play toward*
The Senator *alluded* to a possible increase in federal spending for higher education while giving a speech at the Community College the other day.
syn: hint

COLLUSION (kə lōō´ zhən) *n.* A secret agreement for wrong or unlawful purposes
L. con, "together," + ludus = *playing together*
Such financial fraud would not have been possible without massive *collusion* between the company and its accounting firm.
syn: connivance

INTERLUDE (in´ tər lōōd) *n.* Period between two events or scenes
L. inter, "between," + ludus = *playing between*
The musical *interlude* between acts three and four was arranged by the Harlem Boys' Choir.

RIS
Latin RIDERE, RISUM "to laugh"

DERISIVE (də rīs´ iv) *adj.* Treating with ridicule; scornful
L. de, "down," + risum = *laughing down*
Whenever Pauline spoke of becoming an actress, her father would give her a *derisive* laugh.

Can you think of another common English word from the RIS root?

RISIBLE (riz´ i bəl) *adj.* Drawing laughter or amusement; ridiculous
Even eloquent and moving portions of the film were followed by *risible* lines such as, "Your hair is the color of a lazy afternoon."

FELIC
Latin FELIX "happy, fortunate"

FELICITOUS (fə lis´ i təs) *adj.* Perfectly suitable; appropriate
The *felicitous* union of bananas and chocolate makes the dessert sure-to-please.
syn: apt

INFELICITOUS (in fə lis´ i təs) *adj.* Unfortunate; unhappy
L. in, "not," + felix = *not happy*
By an *infelicitous* turn of events, the man Jesse shot on the road was his own brother.

FELICITY (fə lis´ i tē) *n.* Happiness; bliss
Mary Ann's friends tried to comfort her by saying that today's disaster would only make any later *felicity* seem greater.

The introduction of ELECTRICITY filled the people with a sense of FELICITY.

▥ *The English word felic-itations comes from the same root, means "con-gratulations" and is sometimes included on graduation and birthday cards.*

EXERCISES - UNIT NINETEEN

Exercise I. Complete the sentence in a way that shows you understand the meaning of the italicized vocabulary word.

1. The idea that Daniel would run a marathon was *ludicrous* because…

2. When Alex mentioned "The Lady in the Harbor with the Torch," he was *alluding* to…

3. The defense attorney was accused of *collusion* with the mob boss when…

4. An *interlude* between the second and third acts gave the orchestra a chance to…

5. Peter's *derisive* tone of voice as he described the tennis match let us know he thought…

6. Craig found the council's proposal so *risible* that…

7. An *infelicitous* turn of events before the softball game led to…

8. The *felicity* of the day Mike finally got his degree was like…

9. No marriage could ever have seemed more *felicitous* than Elaine and Darien's, because…

Exercise II. Fill in the blank with the best word from the choices below. One word will not be used.

> ludicrous   derisive   infelicitous   felicitous

1. Mike agreed to wear the frankfurter costume even though he found the idea _____.

2. Dialing the wrong number turned out to be a(n) _____ mistake when the person on the other end agreed to join me for dinner.

3. As he described the actions of his incompetent camp leader, James' tone went from disapproving to _____.

Fill in the blank with the best word from the choices below. One word will not be used.

> allude   infelicitous   collusion   risible

4. The film does _____ to the recent war in a few scenes, but there is no open mention of any current events.

5. In light of the food shortage in many parts of the world, Chef Pat's televised dumping of tons of fast food seems bizarre and a little _____.

6. Although Roger had never considered himself unlucky, a series of _____ accidents was enough to convince him otherwise.

Fill in the blank with the best word from the choices below. One word will not be used.

collusion   interludes   derisive   felicity

7.   The embezzlement case was turned upside down when several investigators were discovered to be in _____ with the suspected thieves.

8.   After the briefest of _____, the boys at the detention camp were ordered back to their ditch-digging.

9.   Rabbi Waldman, having said a few words on the _____ of the occasion, gave the newlyweds his blessing.

Exercise III. Choose the set of words that best completes the sentence.

1.   The aging author refers with _____ fury to younger writers' "_____ belief that they can compete with the great masters."
     A.   risible; felicitous
     B.   derisive; ludicrous
     C.   ludicrous; derisive
     D.   infelicitous; risible

2.   The poisoning was either the result of _____ between family members or a(n) _____ result of an allergy unknown to the deceased.
     A.   collusion; infelicitous
     B.   felicity; risible
     C.   felicity; ludicrous
     D.   interlude; derisive

3.   The current coach's attempt to _____ to great figures from the college's past revealed a _____ ignorance of his own inadequate performance.
     A.   allude; risible
     B.   collusion; felicitous
     C.   allude; infelicitous
     D.   interlude; derisive

4.   The garden's _____ meeting of natural splendor and human ingenuity makes it a lovely place to spend a quiet _____ between busy working hours.
     A.   ludicrous; felicity
     B.   derisive; collusion
     C.   felicitous; interlude
     D.   risible; infelicitous

Exercise IV. Complete the sentence by inferring information about the italicized word from its context.

1. Joshua's body language reinforces his *derisive* attitude; he may be doing things like…

2. If Fred is charged with being in *collusion* with a local crime leader, the attorney who prosecutes him will probably try to prove it by…

3. When the fisherman explains his *ludicrous* new plan for catching more lobsters, his friends will probably respond by…

Exercise V. Fill in the blank with the word from the Unit that best completes the sentence, using the root we supply as a clue. Then, answer the questions that follow the paragraphs.

Ludwig van Beethoven was born in 1770 in Bonn, Germany, to a family of musicians. His gift for music was evident early, and his father taught him the violin and the clavier (an early keyboard instrument). At the age of twelve, having studied the organ and the music of J.S. Bach with a concertmaster, Beethoven became the rehearsal conductor for a German court orchestra, playing operas and orchestral works for the local nobility. He was also composing and publishing music with regularity at this time.

In spite of his seriousness as a student, Beethoven loved a joke. When he was 15, he was the organ accompanist to a singer who had antagonized him. In an effort to make the singer look _____(LUD), Beethoven modulated the notes he played and threw the performer off key during an important performance. Two years later, though, Beethoven's life took a more serious turn, and he traveled to Vienna, an important and highly cultured city. During his _____(LUD) in the Austrian capital, Beethoven met Mozart and Haydn, two leading composers who were impressed by his musical genius. Returning to Germany, Beethoven became friendly with a young nobleman of some musical distinction, Count Waldstein. The Count helped Beethoven with the gift of a good piano and also _____(LUD) with other officials to secure allowances for Beethoven from the court. Seven years later,

Beethoven made the Count famous by dedicating a piano sonata to him.

In 1792, when Beethoven was 22, he again left for Vienna, where he lived for the rest of his life. Following a period of study with Haydn, he became a fixture of the court, which was the center of musical appointments and opportunities. Though he was quite successful as an orchestral musician and composer, his manners were graceless, and he demanded a great deal of attention. He made _____(RIS) comments about the music of others and behaved rudely to other musicians and composers, largely cutting himself off from the give-and-take of the musical community. To further complicate matters, his career as a performer was compromised and eventually ended by his growing deafness. By 1818, he had lost his hearing completely, which only added to his social isolation.

Beethoven's work is painstakingly constructed, with layers of tones and innovative musical structures. He was a perfectionist, and he drove himself to produce finely polished works that expressed his deepest feelings. He was also a prolific composer, with more than 250 publications to his credit, including one opera, nine symphonies, and numerous piano works. He is frequently cited as the composer who most completely exemplifies the clarity and symmetry of the Classical style.

1.   Which sentence best summarizes Beethoven's career as a performer?
      A.   He was a minstrel, traveling through most European capitals.
      B.   He was a famous tenor in operatic productions.
      C.   He was a brilliant player, concentrating on piano and organ.
      D.   He rarely played in public and was known only as a composer.
      E.   He grew deaf later in life.

2.   Beethoven's social life was limited because
      A.   he drank too much and never bathed.
      B.   he was a practical joker and demanded special foods and favors.
      C.   his bad manners annoyed people, and he was handicapped by deafness.
      D.   he insisted on playing the piano at every gathering and sang off-key at parties.
      E.   Both B and C

3.   Which sentence is most accurate about Beethoven's early years?
      A.   He was recognized as a boy genius, but he wasted his teachers' time.
      B.   His family was rich, so he had many teachers.
      C.   His family was poor, so his only teacher was his father.
      D.   His musical gifts were recognized early, and he studied hard.
      E.   He was taught by J.S. Bach.

4.   Beethoven's fame as a composer is secure because
      A.   he excelled at writing many kinds of music.
      B.   he wrote only for the organ, and he has few competitors in that field.
      C.   his many operas are performed all over the world.
      D.   he knew that people get bored easily, so he only wrote short pieces.
      E.   he composed music even though he was deaf.

Exercise VI. Drawing on your knowledge of roots and words in context, read the following selection and define the *italicized* words. If you cannot figure out the meaning of the words on your own, look them up in a dictionary.

   The presidential debate took on a *ludic* form last night when the candidate was asked about her plan for stemming the rising unemployment rate. She responded with "I am going to start by making sure I get a job at the White House." Many in the crowd responded with cheers and laughs, as her opponent offered his *felicitations* on a joke well told.

UNIT TWENTY

STRING, STRICT, STRAIN
Latin STRINGERE, STRICTUM "to bind, to press"

An astringent (ad, "toward," + stringere) is a substance that makes blood or tissue contract. The most common use of astringents is in facial cleansers.

STRINGENT (strin´ jənt) *adj.* Tightly limiting; severe
Stringent security measures were passed by the Senate following the terrorist attacks of September 11th.
syn: rigid   ant: loose

STRICTURE (strik´ shər) *n.* A limit or restraint
The *strictures* placed upon citizens by the government included a seven o'clock curfew.
syn: restriction

PRESTIGE (pres tēzh´) *n.* Recognition or respect from others
L. pre, "before," + stringere = *to press before*
Although the award brought him much *prestige* in literary circles, Ray did not value it as much as his own satisfaction with his work.

CONSTRAIN (kən strān´) *v.* To hold in or keep back by force; confine
L. con, "together," + stringere = *to press together*
In order to *constrain* the growth of the bacteria, doctors used a strong antibiotic.

They used belts to CONSTRAIN the CONS on the TRAIN.

STRUS
Latin TRUDERE, TRUSUM "to thrust, push out"

ABSTRUSE (ab strōōs´) *adj.* Difficult to grasp or learn
L. ab, "away from," + trusum = *pushed away from, hidden*
Some of the book's subject matter is so *abstruse* that even experts have a hard time making sense of it.

OBTRUSIVE (ob trōō´ siv) *adj.* Drawing attention to oneself in a negative way; unpleasantly noticeable
L. ob, "in the way of," trusum = *thrust in the way of*
The decorator is looking for a wallpaper that will accentuate the room's colors without being *obtrusive*.

INTRUSIVE (in trōō´siv) *adj.* Forcing into without invitation; inappropriately personal
L. in, "in," + trusum = *thrusting into*
Fed up with the host's *intrusive* questions, the interviewee began answering, "None of your business."

RIG, RECT, ROIT
Latin RIGERE, RECTUM "to stand up, be straight"

RECTIFY (rek´ tə fī) *v.* To put straight; correct or adjust
The panel spent the afternoon brainstorming ways to *rectify* the injustice it had caused.

INCORRIGIBLE (in kôr´ i jə bəl) *adj.* Not capable of being made better; habitually wicked
L. in, "not," + con, "with," + rigere = *not able to be straightened with*
Even the most *incorrigible* career criminals seemed to change their ways after graduating from the program.

RECTITUDE (rek´ tə tōōd) *n.* Good moral character; ethical quality
Though known as a priest of the utmost *rectitude*, Father Patrick sometimes doubted himself.
syn: uprightness

ADROIT (ə droit´) *adj.* Skillful and clever
French, *adroit*, "to the right," from ad, "toward," + *dis*, "apart," + rectus
No one was more *adroit* than my father at managing the daily disasters that occurred in a six-person household.
syn: dexterous   *ant:* clumsy

▥ *In early French, as in Latin, right-handedness was associated with positive qualities, while left-handedness was frowned upon. The Latin words for "right" (dextra) and "left" (sinistra) give us dexterity, a good quality, and* sinister, *which means "evil, promising doom." The French* droit *meant, "right-handed, direct, straightforward," and gives us adroit; a French word of Germanic origins,* gauche, *meant "lefthanded, clumsy" and gives us our* gauche *(meaning "graceless, awkward").*

EXERCISES - UNIT TWENTY

Exercise I. Complete the sentence in a way that shows you understand the meaning of the italicized vocabulary word.

1.   Because she assumed that the university had *stringent* entrance requirements, Stacy...

2.   The number of advertisements that could be aired in a certain time period was *constrained* by...

3.   In spite of the *strictures* put in place by the Art Academy, the painter was able to...

4.   Certain passages of the medieval treatise were so *abstruse* that...

5.   Franklin found the large picture in the living room *obtrusive* because...

6.   Warren reacted to the reporter's *intrusive* questions by...

7.   Samantha's father often said she was *incorrigible* because...

8.   The local businessman's *rectitude* made him a natural choice for...

9.   Rob's *adroit* management of the robbery at his store...

10.   The only way for Earl to *rectify* the problems he had caused at the zoo was...

11.   The incident involving the oil tanker may damage the company's *prestige*, because...

Exercise II. Fill in the blank with the best word from the choices below. One word will not be used.

stringent   adroit   obtrusive   incorrigible   rectify

1.   Only an unusually _____ pianist can handle the tricky tempo changes and shifts in key demanded by the composer.

2.   _____ fast food eaters will sneak back to the drive-thru again and again, in spite of doctors' orders.

3.   In response to the growing traffic fatality rate, the advisory board urged more _____ seatbelt regulations.

4.   Though he was supposed to provide soft background music, the pianist chose _____ songs that forced people to stop in the middle of their conversations.

Fill in the blank with the best word from the choices below. One word will not be used.

intrusive   prestige   rectified   abstruse   constrained

5.   Thaddeus imagined that an award-winning novel would bring him more _____ than a modeling contract.

6.   The bank manager explained to Lucy that the current financial situation _____ him to a limited fund from which he could lend money.

7.   Bivens, the butler, managed to provide friendly and personal service to his employers without being _____.

8.   Few works deal with more _____ aspects of history than this recently published seven-volume collection.

Fill in the blank with the best word from the choices below. One word will not be used.

obtrusive   incorrigible   rectitude   stricture

9.   Liza, a(n) _____ speeder, was warned that if she got one more ticket, her license would be revoked.

10.   In light of the severe _____ of his society, the artist managed a remarkable freedom of expression.

11.   According to Sister Henrietta, saints are people of such _____ that the idea of wrongdoing never even occurs to them.

Exercise III. Choose the set of words that best completes the sentence.

1.   A(n) _____ cheat like Ollie will disregard even the most _____ penalties for his behavior.
      A.   incorrigible; stringent
      B.   obtrusive; adroit
      C.   abstruse; stringent
      D.   incorrigible; adroit

2.   The _____ imposed by the Church were meant to inspire people to greater _____, not drive them to break rules out of exasperated rebellion.
      A.   rectitudes; stricture
      B.   prestiges; rectitude
      C.   strictures; rectitude
      D.   strictures; prestige

3.   In addition to the increased _____, Tim's artistic success brought _____ reporters to the door and even to the windows.
       A.   prestige; intrusive
       B.   rectitude; obtrusive
       C.   stricture; incorrigible
       D.   prestige; adroit

4.   "I think you will find," said the Professor, "that such _____ research topics will _____ you to one very small part of the library."
       A.   intrusive; rectify
       B.   rectify; constrain
       C.   adroit; rectify
       D.   abstruse; constrain

5.   An _____ photographer can take close-up shots of the bride and groom without being _____.
       A.   obtrusive; adroit
       B.   abstruse; stringent
       C.   adroit; obtrusive
       D.   incorrigible; intrusive

Exercise IV. Complete the sentence by inferring information about the italicized word from its context.

1. If Tanya finds the policies of the office where she works too *stringent*, she may suggest that…

2. If the king does not *rectify* the injustices done by his father, he may find that…

3. A lecturer on extremely *abstruse* topics may notice his audience doing things like…

Exercise V. Fill in the blank with the word from the Unit that best completes the sentence, using the root we supply as a clue. Then, answer the questions that follow the paragraphs.

Alcatraz Island, dedicated to imprisoning society's most _____(RIG) criminals, carried the theory of prisoner isolation to new extremes during its 30-year history. In 1775, the Spanish explorer Juan Manuel de Ayala gave Alcatraz its name, which means "pelican" or "strange bird." The U.S. Army later built a fortress and then a military prison on the island. The Federal Bureau of Prisons acquired the island in 1933, when the government was attempting to show it was serious about halting rampant crime in post-Depression America.

The isolated prison provided a _____(STRING) and secure environment for the nation's most notorious criminals, including mob boss Al Capone and Robert Stroud, later known as the "Birdman of Alcatraz." They and others proved the need for more segregation than standard prisons of the time could provide.

Capone, who was in the first group of prisoners to arrive, was transferred from the federal prison in Atlanta in August, 1934. While in Atlanta, Capone had continued to run his Chicago crime organization from his prison cell without the authorities becoming too _____ (STRUS). He had been in constant contact with mob members who took up residence in nearby hotels, and he was _____ (RUIT) at enlisting fellow inmates and prison guards as personal servants. Once behind bars at Alcatraz, however, all that changed. Capone was assigned difficult, menial prison jobs and given no special treatment. He found the Alcatraz atmosphere much more _____(STRAIN).

In 1909, Stroud was incarcerated in the U.S. Penitentiary on McNeil Island after being sentenced to 12 years for manslaughter. Three years later, though, he was transferred to Leavenworth for viciously attacking a fellow inmate. In 1916, Stroud attacked and killed a custodial worker in front of 2,000 other inmates and was sentenced to death.

His mother pleaded for his life, and in 1920 President Woodrow Wilson commuted his sentence to life in prison. While at Leavenworth, Stroud developed an interest in studying birds. Initially, the hobby was encouraged, but Stroud eventually began to violate prison rules and regulations, and further action was taken. He was packed up in the middle of the night and shipped to Alcatraz in 1942, where he spent the next 17 years in isolation, segregated from the rest of the prison population.

At Alcatraz, some prisoners were given relative freedom while at work, because officials believed that the frigid, choppy waters separating Alcatraz from the mainland would hinder escape attempts. Indeed, though prisoners tried to escape 14 times, none got off the island alive.

Alcatraz closed in 1963 after the federal government determined that it was too costly to operate (one reason was that all food and supplies, including water, had to be shipped to the island by boat). In the end, the island's isolation became its downfall.

1. Which sentence best sums up the main idea of the passage?
    A. Alcatraz Island's isolation made it the perfect spot to house the nation's most incorrigible criminals.
    B. Alcatraz proved that prisoners need rehabilitation, not just isolation.
    C. The federal government remodeled its prison system to deal with the violent crime of post-Depression America.
    D. Alcatraz prison housed some of the nation's most notorious criminals during its 30-year history.

2. Al Capone was moved from the Atlanta prison because
    A. he enlisted guards to do work for him.
    B. he had too much access to his outside life.
    C. he was a danger to other prisoners.
    D. officials wanted him to die far away.

3. Robert Stroud was moved to Alcatraz because
    A. he killed a custodian in front of 2,000 prisoners.
    B. he had violent tendencies.
    C. he attacked a fellow inmate at McNeil penitentiary.
    D. his study of birds led him to violate prison rules.

4. Alcatraz prison closed because
    A. the prison needed too many repairs.
    B. too many prisoners died trying to escape.
    C. the federal government reformed its prison system in the 1960s.
    D. the prison's isolation made it too expensive to operate.

Exercise VI. Drawing on your knowledge of roots and words in context, read the following selection and define the *italicized* words. If you cannot figure out the meaning of the words on your own, look them up in a dictionary. Note that *ex* means "out" and *con* means "together."

Strange formations *extruded* from the walls and ceilings of the cave, suggesting that the area had not been disturbed by human beings for thousands of years. Ducking and twisting to avoid these fingers of rock, the explorers made their way through a narrow passage and emerged in an open chamber. To their shock, they saw that the walls were covered in gloriously elaborate paintings. "When I laid eyes upon these ancient treasures, I felt my chest *constrict*," said one of the archaeologists later. "Their beauty just took my breath away."

UNIT TWENTY-ONE

SAT
Latin SATIS "enough"

INSATIABLE (in sā´ shə bəl) *adj.* Never satisfied or full; always desiring more
L. in, "not," + satis = *not able to get enough*
Bill's *insatiable* appetite for comic books led him to read over a hundred a week.
syn: unquenchable

SATIETY (sə tī´ ə tē) *n.* Condition of being too full or too satisfied
Having eaten to the point of *satiety*, the children felt sleepy and a little sick.

ASSET (a´ sət) *n.* Something of value; a resource
L. ad, "towards," + satis = *(that which helps) towards enough*
Because of her speed, intelligence, and good heart, Michelle is a real *asset* to her basketball team.
syn: credit   *ant*: liability

PLEN
Latin PLENUS "full"

PLENARY (ple´ nə rē) *adj.* Full or complete
Though he will only be in office a short time, the temporary governor will have *plenary* power over the state legislature.
syn: total

PLENIPOTENTIARY (plen i pō ten´ shē ər ē) *adj.* Having full power or authority
L. plenus + potens, "powerful" = *fully powerful*
As a *plenipotentiary* representative of the Spanish nation, the diplomat was authorized to make any decision on behalf of Spain.

⊪ *Based on your knowledge of this root, what do you think* replenish *means literally?*

VAC, VOID
Latin VACUUS "empty"

DEVOID (də voyd´) *adj.* Lacking; completely empty
L. de, "from," + vacuus = *empty from, empty of*
Many survivors of the war report that their lives are now *devoid* of any pleasure.
ant: replete

VACUOUS (vak´ yōō əs) *adj.* Empty of intelligence; stupid
The *vacuous* expression that Kirk wore throughout the school day revealed how little interest he took in his own education.
syn: vacant

VACUITY (va kyōō´ ə tē) *n.* A lack; emptiness or absence
Where Lisa once had a loving heart, she now has an emotional *vacuity*.

Empty-headers march in support of VACUITY.

VAN
Latin, VANUS "empty"

EVANESCENT (ə və nə´ sənt) *adj.* Quickly disappearing; fleeting
L. ex, "out," + vanus = *to empty out, to vanish from*
Evanescent moments of joy leave us longing for lasting happiness.
syn: short-lived

VAUNTED (vawn´ təd) *adj.* Boasted about; too highly praised
For all his *vaunted* achievements on the basketball court, RJ was just a regular guy.

▥ *A vacuole is an empty cavity, often surrounded by a membrane, in the cytoplasm of a cell. In a plant, the vacuoles fill with water, helping to keep the plant upright. When its vacuoles are empty, a plant wilts.*

EXERCISES - UNIT TWENTY-ONE

Exercise I. Complete the sentence in a way that shows you understand the meaning of the italicized vocabulary word.

1.   The general was invested with *plenary* authority because…

2.   Andrew found out how *evanescent* first romances could be when…

3.   Manuel's *insatiable* appetite for candy bars led him to…

4.   Rather than being an *asset* to the volunteer organization, Rona…

5.   Congress made the President a *plenipotentiary* delegate at the negotiations because…

6.   When our host returned from the telephone call *devoid* of all previous enthusiasm, we suspected that…

7.   The *vaunted* wealth of the thriving city turned out to be…

8.   Vera's *vacuous* demeanor as she watched television told us that…

9.   A *vacuity* of art and culture in the small town resulted in…

10.   Only after the sharks had reached *satiety* did they…

Exercise II. Fill in the blank with the best word from the choices below. One word will not be used.

insatiable   evanescent   plenary   vaunted

1.   Do you believe that first romances can last a lifetime, or that they are as _____ as the dew on the grass?

2.   The council invoked its _____ authority to make one of the most significant decisions of our time.

3.   Samantha's _____ desire for success and power led her to become a CEO at a young age.

Fill in the blank with the best word from the choices below. One word will not be used.

vaunted   plenipotentiary   vacuous   satiety   vacuity

4. Media coverage of the band was so overabundant that even the group's biggest fans reached _____.

5. All of the new manager's _____ improvements to the team made little difference in the season's final rankings.

6. The sheriff named a _____ deputy who would be authorized to act in the name of the police chief.

7. Sherry's _____ gaze gave no hint that she was paying attention, let alone comprehending the lecture material.

Fill in the blank with the best word from the choices below. One word will not be used.

vacuity   devoid   asset   plenary

8. A good bedside manner is a crucial _____ for a pediatrician.

9. The movie was criticized for being _____ of meaningful content and depending on flashy special effects to please its audience.

10. Critics warn that television is now filling the emotional _____ left when busy parents cannot spend time with their children.

Exercise III. Choose the set of words that best completes the sentence.

1. Being _____ of any natural math ability, Donna assumed she was not a(n) _____ to her company's marketing department.
   A. evanescent; asset
   B. devoid; asset
   C. plenary; vacuity
   D. vacuous; satiety

2. Joanne complained that our _____ system of television networks, once a source of tremendous pride, now delivers meaningless information until our minds are beyond _____.
   A. satiety; plenary
   B. asset; devoid
   C. vacuity; plenipotentiary
   D. vaunted; satiety

3.   A(n) _____ official was nominated to fill the _____ of authority left by the departing
     president.
     A.   devoid; satiety
     B.   plenipotentiary; vacuity
     C.   evanescent; asset
     D.   satiety; devoid

4.   The business group's bid for _____ control over the negotiations revealed a(n) _____
     desire for power that was quite disturbing.
     A.   vaunted; plenary
     B.   plenary; insatiable
     C.   devoid; evanescent
     D.   devoid; vacuous

5.   Despite her _____ appearance, Annabelle had experienced a few _____moments of under-
     standing and clarity.
     A.   devoid; insatiable
     B.   plenary; satiety
     C.   vaunted; devoid
     D.   vacuous; evanescent

Exercise IV. Complete the sentence by inferring information about the italicized word from its context.

1.   As a *plenipotentiary* representative of the airline corporation, Albert was authorized to…

2.   We could tell that the baby eagles had reached *satiety* when…

3.   The economist's much-*vaunted* plan for the downtown area was supposed to…

**Exercise V. Fill in the blank with the word from the Unit that best completes the sentence, using the root
       we supply as a clue. Then, answer the questions that follow the paragraphs.**

When the U.S. economy falters and international events grow more dire, millions of people turn to television's latest form of escapism: _____(VAC) shows that feature ordinary people in unscripted situations. America's appetite for watching clueless people pick potential mates or consume repulsive food has grown_____(SAT). These shows are an example of the moral decline of our society. Fast-food television fills us up and distracts us, but fails to nourish us or help us grow.

Edward R. Murrow once wrote that television "can teach, it can illuminate; yes, and it can even inspire. But it can do so only to the extent that humans are determined to use it to those ends. Otherwise it is merely wires and lights in a box." Unfortunately, the second eventuality has come to pass. The TV industry is rushing to cram more reality TV shows into production.

Humans' natural voyeuristic tendencies have come together with a highly competitive television market and relaxed attitudes about television content to create the perfect atmosphere for reality TV. And with competition increasing, shows will only become more daring and dangerous. In fact, one 1995 murder was attributed to a sensationalistic episode of "The Jenny Jones Show."

It's a sad reality that hit television shows today make celebrities out of people willing to sacrifice their privacy and dignity for a chance at making a fast buck. We've become so _____(VOID) of self-respect and desperate for our 15 minutes of fame that we ignore the real people and real events in our own lives.

Frank Farley, past president of the American Psychological Association and Temple University teacher, says television shows, tabloids, and other reality-type media promote the idea that it's perfectly fine to express oneself without inhibition. This may be a factor in the high levels of anger and expressions of rage we see in our society today. If we are to take back our society, improve television programming, and halt worship of instantaneous fame and fortune, we need to tune back into our families, loved ones, and communities by spending time getting to know real people who are important in our lives.

1. What is the main idea of this passage?
    A. Reality TV is a distraction from today's political and social problems.
    B. Reality TV is a reflection of our society's moral decline.
    C. In an effort to stay competitive, reality TV shows may grow more violent.
    D. Watching reality TV encourages people to act with fewer inhibitions.

2. The author of this passage would probably agree with which statement below?
    A. TV viewers have only themselves to blame for poor programming.
    B. Violent television leads to violence in society.
    C. Networks should not provide escapist programming.
    D. All television has become exploitative.

3. Frank Farley condemns reality shows because
    A. they exploit participants.
    B. they promote violence.
    C. they detract attention from more important pursuits.
    D. they encourage people to act without inhibition.

4. Reality TV actually began
    A. with Edward R. Murrow's comments.
    B. when networks realized the monetary savings available.
    C. when "humans' natural voyeuristic tendencies" reached their peak.
    D. The article does not specify when.

Exercise VI. Drawing on your knowledge of roots and words in context, read the following selection and define the *italicized* words. If you cannot figure out the meaning of the words on your own, look them up in a dictionary.

Since the current governor has announced his plans to *vacate* the office before the traditional date of election, there may be no governor for several months. The state constitution provides for this sort of emergency by authorizing a special election. A new governor can only be elected at a *plenum* of the central legislature, however; if any members are absent, the vote is invalidated.

UNIT TWENTY-TWO

TENU
Latin TENUS "thin"

ATTENUATE (ə ten´ yōō āt) *v.* To make smaller or less; to weaken
ad, "towards," + tenus = *towards the thin*
Years of hard labor and poor nutrition had *attenuated* Daniel's once large and bulky frame.
syn: to thin   *ant:* increase; amplify

EXTENUATING (ek sten´ yōō āt ing) *adj.* Serving to excuse; lessening the
          seriousness of
The defense attorney tried to point to *extenuating* circumstances that might excuse his client of participating in the robbery.

TENUOUS (ten´ yōō əs) *adj.* Not substantial or strong
Joey realized that his grasp of the complicated musical piece was only *tenuous*, despite hours of practice.
syn: flimsy

My skill at TENNIS is TENUOUS at best.

TEN
Latin TENERE, TENTUM "hold"

PERTINACIOUS (pûr tə nā shəs) *adj.* Holding firmly to; stubborn
L. per, "thoroughly, strongly" + tenere = *holding strongly, clinging*
Norman's *pertinacious* fight for justice led him all the way to the Supreme Court.
syn: unyielding

TENET (ten´ ət) *n.* A principle or belief held as part of a religion or philosophy
The existence of original sin is an essential *tenet* of the Roman Catholic faith.

TENABLE (ten´ ə bəl) *adj.* Able to be defended or supported
The judge asked the prosecutor for *tenable* evidence that Mr. Rockland had committed theft.

🏛 *A lieutenant (French lieu, "place," + tenere) is someone who holds or exercises authority in place of a superior.*

TEND
Latin TENDERE, TENSUM "stretch"

CONTEND (kən tend´) *v.* To argue; to dispute
L. con, "with," + tendere = stretch with
Following the election of 2000, Democratic presidential candidate Al Gore
contended that the voting results of the state of Florida were incorrectly tallied.

OSTENSIBLE (ä sten´ sə bəl) *adj.* Seeming, claimed, or pretended, but usually
        not genuine
L. ob, "in the way of," + tensum = *stretched in the way of*
Rick's *ostensible* reason for visiting was to check on the fish in the pond, but he
was actually looking for money buried in the yard.

PORTEND (pôr tend´) *v.* To be a sign or warning of
L. por, "forth," + tendere = *stretch forth*
Some fringe groups claim that the greenhouse effect *portends* the end of the world.
syn: foretell

DISTEND (dis tend´) *v.* To swell; expand
L. dis, "apart," + tendere = *stretch apart*
When her son's foot began to *distend*, Risa rushed him to the hospital.

TENDENTIOUS (ten den´ shəs) *adj.* Strongly biased
The reporter's strong dislike of the movement for women's rights was clear from
his *tendentious* account of recent protest marches.
syn: partial

> ▥ *Have you noticed the small print on a dollar bill that pronounces it "legal tender"? To tender (from tendere, "stretch out, extend") is to offer or give. Money printed at an authorized facility can legally be tendered for goods and services. The word tender meaning "soft or delicate" comes from a different root, the Latin word tener (meaning "fragile").*

EXERCISES - UNIT TWENTY-TWO

Exercise I. Complete the sentence in a way that shows you understand the meaning of the italicized vocabulary word.

1. Because the water supply had *attenuated*...

2. Although Renee had been rude to many of the people at the party, she cited *extenuating* circumstances such as...

3. A *tendentious* article in the magazine revealed that the author...

4. Even after the mosquitoes had departed, the travelers had to *contend* with...

5. Stephen found certain *tenets* of the Church unacceptable because...

6. Dave was surprised that anyone found the theory *tenable* because...

7. The *ostensible* reason for construction of the new train station was...

8. For a small restaurant, a decrease in customers *portends*...

9. The water balloon had *distended* to the point where it seemed...

10. Jessica's *tenuous* grasp of the subject matter in her advanced physics class led her to...

11. Annabel thinks that her *pertinacious* nature is a result of...

Exercise II. Fill in the blank with the best word from the choices below. One word will not be used.

tenuous	extenuating	distended	tenet	pertinacious

1. Nathan's _____ insistence on a recount of the student council votes eventually wore down his opponents.

2. The dam had _____ and looked ready to burst at any moment.

3. Professor Witt reaffirmed his belief in the fundamental _____ of his philosophy.

4. Without strong evidence to support her claims, the lawyer's argument will seem rather _____.

Fill in the blank with the best word from the choices below. One word will not be used.

tenable   attenuate   contended   extenuating   portended

5. The theories of the weight-loss guru were found to be _____ when thousands of dieters reported overnight success.

6. Commentators wondered if the boxer's early loss _____ a decline in the career of the great champ.

7. Though all the evidence indicates that Joel was responsible for the attack, I feel sure there must be some _____ factors that explain his actions.

8. In response to accusations of fraud, the company executive _____ that he was utilizing a new investment scheme.

Fill in the blank with the best word from the choices below. One word will not be used.

ostensible   tenet   tendentious   attenuate

9. A careless observer might mistake Alan's _____ motivation for his actual one.

10. Marvin's _____ debating style tended to divide his audience immediately.

11. Lonnie was determined not to let fatigue and distraction _____ her focus.

Exercise III. Choose the set of words that best completes the sentence.

1. Sally _____ with _____ ferocity that she will get to her sister's recital even if she has to walk the whole twenty miles.
   A. contends; extenuating
   B. portends; tenuous
   C. attenuates; pertinacious
   D. contends; pertinacious

2. The bodies of the zoo animals had been stretched and _____ by disease, and their food supply had _____ months ago.
   A. distended; attenuated
   B. ostensible; portended
   C. tenuous; contended
   D. attenuated; portended

3. Though the principal accepts Carmen's illness as _____ in her absence from school today, he fears that her recent pattern of truancy _____ greater problems for her in the future.
   A. extenuating; portends
   B. ostensible; contends
   C. distended; attenuates
   D. tenable; tendentious

4.   The _____ of the cult prohibit contact with outsiders, for the _____ reason that anyone not in the group is a "corrupter."
      A.   tenets; tendentious
      B.   tenets; ostensible
      C.   attenuations; tenuous
      D.   extenuations; pertinacious

5.   A rather uncertain and _____ claim to political supremacy became the basis for a(n) _____ and bitterly divisive campaign.
      A.   distended; contended
      B.   ostensible; extenuating
      C.   tendentious; ostensible
      D.   tenuous; tendentious

Exercise IV. Complete the sentence by inferring information about the italicized word from its context.

1.   If Mark's mother considers *extenuating* circumstances before she punishes Mark for crashing the car, she probably thinks about things like…

2.   When the Surgeon General calls a shocking new claim by researchers "*tenuous* at best," he probably thinks the researchers should…

3.   When the supply of medicines to the army camp *attenuates*, the soldiers may find that…

Exercise V. Fill in the blank with the word from the Unit that best completes the sentence, using the root we supply as a clue. Then, answer the questions that follow the paragraphs.

During the late centuries B.C.E., free Roman citizens were categorized as either patricians or plebeians. The patricians possessed wealth, power, and the right to vote; therefore, they retained the prerogative to interpret and modify laws in a manner befitting themselves. Plebeians, however, held none or very few of these privileges, which resulted in an _____(TEND) absence of rights and legal protection for them. _____(TEND) that the government had deprived them of their rights, the plebeians united and threatened to secede from the Empire, which, strangely, has had a profound effect on the development of numerous legal systems worldwide.

A group of ten elected Roman officials clarified the existing laws and ordered their inscription onto tablets. The law code was thereafter referred to as the Twelve Tables. This act established an impartial, written code of law which replaced the previous system wherein the unrecorded laws, their implications, and their consequences varied according to the patrician judges' interpretations and interests. The new codified laws enabled patricians and plebeians alike to receive equal legal protection and provided for fair trials with just punishments, rather than arbitrary sentences handed down by biased judges.

In a plight similar to the plebeians', the early American colonists suffered under Great Britain's tyrannical control, and they demanded rights, eventually threatening secession. When a _____(TEN) Britain failed to satisfy their demands, civilian and military leaders representing the colonies endorsed the Declaration of Independence, which enumerated Britain's offenses, the reasons for secession, and the basic human rights that the King of England had proscribed. Having won the war with Great Britain, the colonists needed to establish a democratic leadership that served two purposes: first, to confer rights to all citizens, regardless of their socioeconomic status; and second, to protect the country from the future threat of tyrannical control. Consequently, the states agreed to ratify the 1787 Philadelphia Constitution, but only if the Bill of Rights was added.

The ten Amendments in the Bill of Rights, modeled after the Twelve Tables, prohibited violations of individual rights and provided measures that precluded totalitarianism. Like the Twelve Tables, the Bill of Rights placed significant emphasis on trial procedures, ensuring the right to a speedy trial by an impartial jury, freedom from double jeopardy, and the right to counsel. Perhaps the most important Amendment was the First, which provided freedom of speech and the right to petition for change in government. In giving individuals a right to express opinions and to challenge decisions, the document prevented the abuse of power. Ironically, such abuse had been the causal factor in the creation of both the Roman and the American legal systems.

1. Which sentence below best sums up the importance of written laws, according to the author?
    A. Societies create numerous laws, and remembering them would be extremely difficult.
    B. Unwritten laws have unwritten consequences, and this enables bias to control legal decisions.
    C. Once laws are written, everyone is required to follow them; ignorance is inexcusable.
    D. A law does not become official until it is written.

2. Why did the plebeians of Rome threaten to secede?
    A. They wanted to develop their own system of government.
    B. The patricians had ignored them for many years.
    C. The patricians had treated them unfairly in the courts.
    D. They objected to the laws written in the Twelve Tables.

3. Which of the following is NOT a similarity between the Twelve Tables and the Bill of Rights?
    A. They both were written in response to unjust leadership.
    B. They both provided fair trial procedures.
    C. They both attempted to end legal bias.
    D. They both were written in response to revolts.

4. What important effect did the Bill of Rights have on the American legal system?
    A. It outlined fair trial procedures.
    B. It gave judges flexibility in interpreting the law.
    C. It reiterated the Declaration of Independence.
    D. It outlined the procedure for impeaching an official.

Exercise V. Fill in the blank with the word from the Unit that best completes the sentence, using the root we supply as a clue. Then, answer the questions that follow the paragraphs. Note that *de* means "away, down," and *per* means "through."

Once hostile relations with the rogue nation had subsided, the United Nations voted as a body to pursue a policy of *détente* towards the new administration. The locks that had been tightly limiting commerce between more developed countries and this small, but resource-rich, nation were loosed, and citizens of the country were once again free to stretch their economic limbs. Suddenly, many foreign-trade issues that had not been *pertinent* during the years of isolation seemed to matter a great deal.

VOCABULARY WORD LIST FOR OTHER BOOKS IN THIS SERIES

Book I

abbreviate
absent
accept
access
aerate
aeronautic
affect
affection
agent
aggressive
agile
alleviate
announce
armament
astrology
astronomical
aura
aurora
barometer
biped
brevity
campaign
campus
capital
captivate
captive
celebration
celebrity
collaborate
command
comment
common
communicate
compass
compassion
conscience
conserve
constellation
convict
cooperate
corporal
corporal
corporation
corps
countless
course
credit
creed
current
cursive
decapitate
decision
deflate
deliver
delude
demand
demented
demilitarized
depend
deposit
describe

diagram
disarm
disaster
discount
disintegrate
distant
domestic
dominate
dominion
donation
donor
effort
elevate
elongate
emancipate
emblem
encamp
engrave
envelop
evaluate
evict
exhilarating
expose
extend
fable
fabulous
factor
feast
festival
festive
fortify
fortress
gradual
grammar
graphic
grave
gravity
hilarity
homicide
hyperventilate
idea
ideal
idealistic
illusion
immune
impersonate
impossible
incredible
inflate
inoperable
insane
inspire
integrate
integrity
intend
interest
invalid
invest
jubilant
jubilee
labor
lax

lease
lever
levitate
liberal
liberate
literal
literate
longitude
lunacy
lunar
lunatic
mandate
manual
manufacture
manuscript
mental
mentality
militant
military
militia
narrate
narrative
object
obliterate
observe
occur
omnipotent
operation
opinion
opinionated
oral
oration
oratory
parable
paragraph
paranoia
pardon
passage
passion
passive
patent
pathetic
patient
pedestal
pedestrian
pendulum
permanent
persona
petrify
possess
precision
present
preserve
pretend
process
program
progress
project
prolong
pronounce
rapid
ravage

ravish
refuge
refugee
regal
regicide
reign
reject
relax
release
remain
respirator
reveal
sanitation
sanity
science
scientific
spirit
state
status
stellar
subscribe
success
suppose
suspend
symbolize
sympathy
terrain
terrestrial
territory
transaction
unveil
valid
value
ventilate
vestment
victor

Book II

abduct
abhor
abundant
accelerate
accumulate
acrophobia
activate
administer
administration
advise
agitate
allergy
amass
ambitious
amputate
annual
anticipate
appreciate
approve
approximate
arrange
aspersion
assault
asset

automatic
automaton
avail
celestial
centennial
chronic
chronology
clarify
clarity
comfort
compass
compose
compute
conceive
condone
conduct
confine
confuse
congratulate
consolidate
constant
contemporary
contract
controversy
convert
cumulative
deceive
decelerate
dedicate
deduct
deify
deity
demarcation
depreciate
deputy
derange
deterrent
diagnosis
differ
digest
disapprove
discourse
disgrace
dislocate
disperse
dispose
durable
duration
edition
elect
enact
enclose
endure
energetic
enforce
ergonomic
evident
exception
excite
exclusive
excursion
executive

exhibit
exhume
expectant
extract
finite
fortitude
gratitude
horrific
horrify
humble
humiliate
humility
hydrophobia
hypothesis
import
important
incite
include
indicate
ingest
inhabit
inscribe
inspect
instant
insular
insulate
insult
intercept
intimidate
invigorate
involve
isolate
issue
journal
legend
locale
marinate
mariner
maritime
massive
method
millennium
minister
ministry
monotheism
nebula
nebulous
neglect
notable
notary
notation
odometer
oppose
optic
optical
optometry
participate
passable
patent
peninsula
period
periodic

phobia
polytheism
precious
prescribe
preside
probation
prognosis
prohibit
prosecution
prosthetic
provide
proximity
ratio
ration
rational
react
recognition
reconnaissance
reduce
redundant
refine
refuse
reinforce
relocate
remarkable
reputation
reside
revise
revolution
revolve
sacred
sacrifice
sanctify
sanctuary
satisfactory
satisfy
sedentary
sequence
single
singular
site
situate
sojourn
solar
solarium
solidarity
solitary
solitude
sparse
statistical
substance
subtract
suffer
suggest
supervise
support
surround
suspicious
syndicate
synthetic
tempo
temporary
terrify
terrorize
theology

timid
timorous
topic
tradition
transcribe
transfer
transit
universal
valiant
valor
vigorous
vista

Book III

abjure
abstain
accord
adept
affable
affiliate
affluent
agenda
alias
alienate
allegation
alleviate
alteration
altercation
alternate
amble
ambulatory
amiable
amicable
analogous
animosity
anonymous
antagonist
antagonize
antebellum
antibiotic
antonym
aptitude
aristocracy
assonance
audit
auditory
bellicose
belligerence
benefactor
benevolent
benign
bibliophile
biodegradable
bureaucrat
cadence
casualty
cede
circumspect
cognitive
cognizant
collapse
concession
confound
conjure
consecutive

cordial
corporeal
corpulent
courier
decadent
delegate
denomination
deplete
dialogue
dictum
digress
dilate
diminish
discord
disenchanted
dismal
dispel
disposition
dissemble
dissonance
divest
domineering
edict
effigy
elapse
elucidate
enamored
enjoin
enunciate
equanimity
equilibrium
equitable
exacting
execution
expatriate
expedient
figment
filial
formative
genealogy
gradualism
herbivorous
homogenized
homonym
immortalize
impart
impartial
impediment
implement
impose
imprecise
improvise
inalienable
inaudible
incantation
incision
inclusive
incognito
inconclusive
inconsequential
incorporate
incur
indecisive
indicted
ineffable

inept
infantile
infuse
inhibit
iniquity
injunction
invidious
invoke
leaven
legacy
legislative
legitimize
levity
lucid
magnanimous
magnate
magnetic
magnify
malevolent
malicious
maternal
matriculate
matron
megalomaniac
megalopolis
mellifluous
metabolism
metamorphosis
metaphorical
microcosm
microscopic
miniscule
minute
misinformation
monogamy
monolithic
monologue
monopolize
morbid
moribund
mortify
nomenclature
nominal
noxious
omnivorous
partisan
paternal
patricide
patronize
pedagogue
pedant
pedestrian
perceptible
perjury
pernicious
philanthropy
philosophical
phosphorescent
photogenic
phototropic
posit
preamble
precept
preclude
predominant indom-

itable
prefigure
privileged
proactive
progenitor
progeny
prohibit
prologue
pronouncement
propel
prospect
protagonist
providential
provocative
rapacious
rapt
recant
recede
recurrent
reform
regress
rejoinder
relapse
relative
renounce
replete
repulsion
resonant
retinue
revival
revoke
semblance
simulate
sophisticate
sophistry
sophomoric
specter
suffuse
superfluous
superlative
surreptitious
susceptible
sustain
symbiotic
synonymous
tenacious
theocracy
translucent
travesty
unanimous
uniform
unison
vested
vestment
vivacious
vivid
voracious

Book IV

aberrant
abject
acerbic
acquisitive
acrid
acrimonious

adherent
admonition
adverse
advocate
aesthetic
anatomy
anesthetic
annotate
antipathy
apathetic
apolitical
apparition
approbation
arrogant
arrogate
aspect
benediction
cautionary
cautious
circumvent
civic
civility
civilize
clamorous
colloquial
compel
complacent
comportment
compunction
conciliatory
concise
conducive
confer
confide
congress
conjecture
connotation
conscientious
constructive
construe
convene
convoluted
correspond
cosmopolitan
counsel
covenant
credence
credible
credulity
crucial
crucible
crux
culpable
culprit
cursory
declaim
decriminalize
deduce
defer
deference
definitive
deflect
degrade
dejected
demagogue

demographic
denotation
deprecate
derogatory
despondent
destitute
deviate
diaphanous
dictate
diffident
diffuse
diligent
dismissive
disparate
dispute
disreputable
dissolute
dissuade
docile
doctrine
doleful
dolorous
dubious
effervescent
effusive
egress
eloquent
emissary
emote
empathy
envisage
epiphany
epitome
equivocate
errant
erroneous
espouse
evince
evocative
evolve
exacerbate
excise
exclamatory
excruciating
exonerate
expel
expound
extort
facile
facsimile
factotum
fallacious
fallacy
fallible
fervent
fervor
fidelity
fractious
gratuitous
imperative
impervious
impetuous
impetus
imprecation
impulse

impute
incautious
incisive
incoherent
incredulous
incriminate
incursion
indoctrinate
indolent
indubitable
induce
inference
infinite
infinitesimal
inflection
inflexible
infraction
infrastructure
infringe
ingrate
ingratiate
inherent
innovative
inquisitive
insoluble
intact
intemperate
interrogate
intractable
introspective
invincible
irrational
locution
malediction
mea culpa
motif
motive
novel
novice
obviate
onerous
onus
pandemic
pathos
penultimate
perspicacious
persuasion
petulant
phenomenon
placebo
placid
politicize
precarious
precaution
precursor
premonition
prescient
presentiment
primacy
primal
primeval
proffer
proficient
profuse
proliferate
proponent

protracted
provincial
punctilious
pungent
purported
rationale
rationalize
recollect
reconcile
recourse
recrimination
redoubtable
remiss
repose
reprobate
reprove
requisition
resolute
restitution
retort
retract
retrospective
revert
sacrilege
sentient
sentiment
sentinel
stature
subvert
sycophant
tactile
tangible
temper
temperance
tome
tortuous
ultimate
ultimatum
unconscionable
viaduct
virile
virtue
virtuoso
visage
voluble

Book V
abominable
abomination
abrasive
accede
acquiesce
adorn
adventitious
ambient
annex
antecedent
appall
appease
append
applicable
appraise
appreciable
apropos
ascertain
assertion

assortment
attrition
auspices
auspicious
beatific
beatitude
belabor
belletrist
candid
candor
catholic
circuitous
colligate
communal
conferment
conflagration
congested
consign
consort
contort
contravene
contrite
corrosive
décor
decorative
decorous
decorum
demonstrative
denounce
depict
depose
desolate
destine
desultory
detrimental
detritus
discern
discomfit
disconcert
disintegrate
disseminate
distort
divulge
ecstasy
effulgent
elaborate
embellish
emblematic
emeritus
entity
erode
essence
euphoria
excommunicate
exert
expendable
extant
exultant
feasible
febrile
felicity
ferment
flagrant
flamboyant
florid
flourish

flourishing
foment
fortuitous
fulminate
germane
germinal
germinate
gestate
gesticulate
hoi polloi
holistic
hyperbole
hypnopedic
hypnotic
impair
impeccable
impending
implicit
importune
in toto
incandescent
incendiary
incense
incommunicado
incorrigible
inexplicable
infelicitous
inflammatory
insignia
insufferable
insurrection
integral
interject
interpose
jocular
jocund
laborious
leniency
lenient
lethargy
liaison
liturgy
magnum opus
malaise
malfeasance
malign
malinger
meritorious
meretricious
misfortune
modus operandi
monosyllabic
monotone
monotonous
munificent
negate
negligent
negligible
nexus
objectify
oblige
ominous
operational
ornate
orthodox
orthography

pacific
pallid
pallor
parcel
parse
parvenu
peccadillo
pejorative
periphery
picturesque
polygamous
polyglot
precedent
predestined
preferential
problematic
propitiate
propitious
quintessence
rapport
raze
rectify
refulgent
remonstrate
remunerate
renounce
repartee
requiem
resignation
resilient
restive
sedition
seminal
serenade
serene
serenity
soliloquy
solipsism
somnambulant
somnolent
sortilege
stanch
stasis
static
staunch
suborn
surfeit
surveillance
suspend
synergy
tortion
totalitarian
totality
transient
transitional
transitory
trite
verdant
verdure
vigil
vigilant
vigilante
vulgar

Vocabulary from Literature

Vocabulary study based on literature enhances the study of both.

- *Reading comprehension increases with an improved vocabulary.*

- *Vocabulary retention improves by showing the relevancy of words in real context.*

- *Improved comprehension of nuances by seeing the words as used by masters of word-craft.*

Integrate Your Vocabulary Program & Literature Lessons to Maximize the Learning from Both

Since entering the profession in the early sixties, I've heard the experts exhorting us to base a study of vocabulary on the literature read in the classroom. This is something very easy to say, but almost impossible for a busy teacher to do. We, however, have just made it feasible by getting the groundwork out of the way.

Whether you wish to develop a vocabulary program based on these words or just use our vocabulary materials as an intro or enhancement to literature study, our reproducibles will do the job.

From the text, we've identified the valuable, but generally unfamiliar, words we thought students should know and constructed exercises to reinforce their meanings; for other, more esoteric, words, we have built a glossary so your class can fully understand these great books.

200735	Great Gatsby, The	$24.95	201046	Holes	$24.95
200892	Huckleberry Finn	$24.95	200627	Night	$24.95
200650	Lord of the Flies	$24.95	200649	Of Mice and Men	$24.95
200818	Scarlet Letter, The	$24.95	201961	Frankenstein	$24.95
200376	To Kill a Mockingbird	$24.95	201962	Tale of Two Cities, A	$24.95
200817	Animal Farm	$24.95	201967	Heart of Darkness	$24.95
200851	Fahrenheit 451	$24.95	202212	Giver, The	$24.95

New titles constantly being added, call or visit our website for current listing.

PRESTWICK HOUSE, INC.

"Everything for the English Classroom!"

P.O. Box 658, Clayton, DE 19938

Call toll-free (800) 932-4593 or

Fax your order to (888) 718-9333

www.prestwickhouse.com